SERVING WITH JOY

A STUDY IN PHILIPPIANS

BY

Stephen A. Grunlan

CHRISTIAN PUBLICATIONS

CAMP HILL, PENNSYLVANIA

Christian Publications
Publishing House of The Christian and Missionary Alliance
3825 Hartzdale Drive, Camp Hill, PA 17011

The mark of ✝ *vibrant faith*

ISBN: 0-87509-371-X
Library of Congress Catalog Card Number: 85-71352

Scripture quotations are from the Holy Bible, New International Version. Copyright © 1973, 1978, International Bible Society. Used by permission of Zondervan Bible Publishers.

Printed in the United States of America

SERVING WITH JOY

Contents

Introduction

*M*any of our churches are similar to the church at Philippi. They were an orthodox church with no major heresies, no great doctrinal disputes and no gross sins. They were faithful to the gospel. Yet it was a church in need of encouragement and instruction.

In this study I have attempted to avoid heavy theological issues and details that are of limited scholarly interest. Rather, I have attempted to look at Paul's practical counsel and draw application for us today.

If most of us were honest, we would have to admit that much of our service for God is motivated by guilt or a sense of duty. We often find ourselves filling slots or serving because "somebody has to do it." That is not, however, what God intended. In this brief letter to the church at Philippi, Paul writes about the joy of service. He uses the words *joy* and *rejoice* more than a dozen times in these four chapters.

As we study this epistle we will discover that Paul's joy was not based on circumstances. In fact, some of his circumstances were rather unpleasant. But his joy was in the Lord and in His service. In our examination of Philippians, we will discover the basis of the joy of service. Paul reveals the excitement and fulfillment of serving Jesus Christ in this challenging epistle. It is my prayer that the study of this epistle might encourage and instruct us in our Christian walk.

The multiplicity of Bible versions available today presents a dilemma to the Christian writer. On which version should he base his study? Since the New International Version seems to be gaining wider acceptance in many evangelical circles, I decided to base the study on that version. I recognize, however, that many of you are using the King James Version or the New American Standard Bible (my personal preference for a study Bible), therefore, when doing word studies, I have included the KJV and NASB renderings when they differ from the NIV.

Finally, I want to thank my wife, Sandra, and our children for their patience with me as I have worked on this project. I am indebted to the numerous scholars whose works I have consulted. I also want to recognize Carol Anderson who has typed this manuscript from my scrawlings on legal pads, corrected my spelling, straightened out my grammar and demonstrated true servanthood.

1

A Hearty Greeting

PHILIPPIANS 1:1-2

A few years ago a fascinating experiment was conducted at a state university. Three groups of agricultural majors were given printed copies of a speech proposing an agricultural policy for the United States. One group was told the speech had been given by the Secretary of Agriculture. The second group was told the candidate for the presidency of the United States from the American Communist Party had given the speech. The third group was told a college freshman had given the speech.

Those students who thought it was a college freshman's speech said the policy was naive. The students who had been told it was the Communist candidate's speech said it would ruin American agriculture. The students who were led to believe the speech had been given by the Secretary of Agriculture said it showed great promise. While all three groups of students had read the same speech, each group believed the speech was given in a different context which led to different interpretations.

SERVING WITH JOY

In order for us to better understand the book of Philippians, we need to know something about the author, the recipients and the circumstances under which the epistle was written. A brief overview of the historical and cultural context of this letter will aid us in our study.

Occupying a hilltop overlooking the Plain of Druma, Philippi was a major city in Macedonia. The ancient name of the city was Krenides, which means springs or fountains. Philip II, the father of Alexander the Great, captured the city in 360 B.C. and named all the springs after himself. Hence, the city became known as Philippi, plural for Philip. After the battle of Pydna in 168 B.C., Philippi came under the rule of the Roman Empire.

The famous battle of Philippi, which ended the Roman Republic, pitted the forces of Marc Antony and Octavius Caesar against the forces of Brutus and Cassius in 42 B.C. In A.D. 31, another famous battle was fought at Philippi when the forces of Antony and Cleopatra were defeated by Octavius and the city received the *ius Italicum*, the "Italic right." This meant that its citizens had the same rights and privileges as persons living on Italian soil.

Philippi was located nine miles inland from the seaport of Neapolis, on the famous Egnatian Way. It was to this city that Paul and Silas first came as they brought the gospel to Macedonia. Paul's vision of a call to Macedonia is recorded in Acts 16:6-10. The ministry of Paul and Silas in Philippi is recorded in Acts 16:11-40.

On their first Sabbath in Philippi, Paul and Silas went outside the city to the river where they met with Jews who had come there to pray. They shared the good news of Jesus Christ, and Lydia, a clothing dealer from Thyatira, responded to the message. She and her household were baptized and became the first believers in Philippi.

As Paul and Silas continued to minister in Philippi, they were followed by a demon-possessed slave girl. When Paul delivered her from the demon, her owners, who made money from the girl's fortunetelling, saw their means of income disappear. Enraged, they had Paul and Silas arrested. The court ordered them beaten and imprisoned. During the night Paul and Silas prayed and sang praises to God as the other prisoners looked on in astonishment.

In the middle of the night an earthquake struck the prison area. The doors of the prison were knocked open and the prisoners' chains loosed. The jailor, assuming all the prisoners had escaped, prepared to kill himself since he knew the penalty for allowing a prisoner to escape was death. Paul saw the jailer and called out for him to stop because all the prisoners were still there. Astonished and trembling, the jailer asked what he must do to be saved. Paul told him that he needed to place his faith in Jesus Christ—he and his family. It is quite possible the jailer and his family had also heard Paul and Silas praying and singing. They responded to the message and were baptized.

The next day the courts ordered Paul and Silas released. After visiting the believers gathered at Lydia's house, they left Philippi and a growing church. On his third missionary journey, Paul again visited the city to exhort and encourage the believers (Acts 20:1-6).

It is to this church that Paul directs his letter. His salutation is typical of the letter-writing style of the Greco-Roman world. Archaeologists have discovered much correspondence from that period, and it usually begins, "So-and-so to so-and-so, I trust you are well. . . ."

SERVANTS

Paul begins, "Paul and Timothy, servants of Christ Jesus." It is interesting to note that Paul does not use the title Apostle in this epistle. Paul claims his apostleship in all of his epistles. Besides Philippians, the only exceptions are First and Second Thessalonians and Philemon. Paul uses his authority as an apostle in his teaching epistles, such as Romans and Ephesians, and his disciplining or correcting epistles, such as First Corinthians and Galatians.

Philippians, however, is a counseling letter. It was written to dear friends (4:15-16). It was written to encourage and build up the believers. Paul does not break any new theological ground nor does he engage in correcting doctrinal or ecclesiastical problems. Rather, he reminds them of basic truths. The theme of this epistle is found in verse 27 of chapter 1, "Conduct yourselves in a manner worthy of the gospel of Christ."

Not only does Paul not claim his apostleship, he calls himself a servant. He uses the Greek word *doulos*, which literally means "one bound to another," sometimes translated bondservant. Historians estimate that at least half of the people living in the Roman Empire during the first century were slaves.

There were primarily three ways one became a slave. The first was to be captured. Prisoners of war who were not killed were made slaves. The second was to be sold by another. It was quite common in that day for parents to sell their children as slaves. The third was to sell themselves. If a person was in debt, he could sell himself as a slave to pay off his debt. This practice was similar to indentured servants in early American history. The difference between these methods of becoming a slave is that the first two involve a person's becoming a slave against his or her will. But the third method involves one's choosing to become a slave. It is a voluntary action.

Paul claims he is a servant and names his master, Jesus Christ. God's Son is addressed by three titles in the New Testament: Lord, Jesus and Christ. The title *Lord* means a ruler with legal authority. It acknowledges the kingship and sovereignty of Christ. The name *Jesus* is, of course, His given name. It is the Greek version of Joshua and means Jehovah saves. It testifies that He came to be the Savior of the world. The title *Christ* is the Greek translation of the Jewish word Messiah. It means the anointed one. This speaks of Jesus' priestly function as He intercedes for us.

Interestingly, when Paul writes that he is a servant, he does not call Jesus the Lord, the most obvious title a servant would use for his master. Paul served Jesus, not because He had the authority, but because Jesus was his Savior and High Priest. Paul served Jesus because Jesus had first served him. In Philippians 2:6-8, Paul says that Jesus Christ became a *doulos* and died for us.

While Jesus Christ has the authority to demand our total allegiance, He reaches out to us in love through the cross and asks us to choose to follow Him. Our motivation for service is not to be unwilling obedience to an irresistible authority, but devotion to a loving Savior. We serve Jesus because He first served us. The bondservants of Jesus Christ serve not from compulsion but from love and gratitude.

In this first verse, there is a question of authorship we should settle. Did Paul *and* Timothy write this letter together? It begins "Paul and Timothy...." The answer is no. From verse 3 on, Paul writes in the first person singular using *I*. In Philippians 2:19-24, he refers to

Timothy in the third person. Verse 1 is only a joint greeting. My wife will frequently write a letter to someone and then close by saying, "Steve and I send our love." I did not write the letter, but was only included in a joint greeting. This is a similar situation.

It will also help us to know where Paul was writing from and under what circumstances. According to verse 13 of the first chapter, he was in prison. Which imprisonment is he referring to? While there is not unanimous agreement among New Testament scholars, most agree that this is Paul's imprisonment in Rome which is recorded at the end of the book of Acts (28:16, 30-31). We will look at this imprisonment in more detail when we study verse 13.

SAINTS

Paul continues his salutation by telling who he is addressing, "To all the saints in Christ Jesus at Philippi. . . ." Some churches limit the term saints to great Christians or the church fathers; however, this is not a biblical use of the word. As someone has said, "There are only two classes of people in the world, the saints and the ain'ts." In the New Testament, saint was the basic term used for speaking about a believer. The word saints is used over 225 times in the New Testament; the word Christian is used only 3 times.

The word saints comes from the same root as the word holy and sanctify. It is the equivalent of the Old Testament word for holy which means "to separate." In essence, the saints are the separated ones. There are two aspects of separation, to be separated from and to be separated to. Saints are to be separated from sin and evil and separated to, or set apart for, God's service.

You are, no doubt, familiar with the test used to see if a person is an optimist or a pessimist. A drinking glass

A Hearty Greeting

containing water to its midpoint is shown to a person. The individual is asked to describe the quantity of water in the glass. If the person is an optimist, she will say the glass is half full. If the person is a pessimist, he will say it is half empty. Obviously, both are correct. It is a matter of which aspect of the glass one wants to emphasize.

So it is with holiness; there is a negative aspect and a positive aspect. There are many specific behaviors the Bible tells us to avoid, as well as the appearance of evil. Unfortunately, it is this negative aspect of holiness that we have generally emphasized. Everyone knows what we are against, but does anyone know what we are for?

While we as saints must be separated from sin, I do not believe many people will be attracted to Christ by what we do not do. People are not looking for something to be against; they are looking for something to be for. We need to emphasize the positive side of holiness. We need to proclaim love, hope, service, forgiveness and abundant life. We have a great message; let us show the world what we are for. Let them see that a saint is not a statue, but a living follower of Jesus Christ.

GRACE

The combination of "grace and peace" was a common Pauline greeting found in most of his epistles. Peter also uses it in both of his epistles and John in his second epistle. This is a Greek-Hebrew greeting combining the Greek greeting *Karis* (grace) with the Hebrew greeting *Shalom* (peace). Since the early church was made up of both Greeks, and Jews, it was common to use both greetings.

Grace, as a pagan Greek greeting, referred to a favor

7

done by one person for another out of pure generosity without any thought of repayment. When Paul uses the greeting grace, he is referring to God's favor to us through Jesus Christ. We are all sinners, both by birth and action (Romans 5:12). The penalty for sin is death or eternal separation from God. God is holy and we have seen that holiness means separation from sin. God in His justice requires a penalty for sin. And God in His love provided the penalty in Jesus Christ (John 3:16). In the case of the pagan Greeks, the favor was done for a friend. In the case of God, it was done for His enemies (Romans 5:8-10). Salvation is offered to us by God in His grace. There is nothing we can do to earn it or repay Him (Ephesians 2:8-9). All we can do is accept it by faith. When we do we become saints.

PEACE

In classical Greek the word peace means "to bind together." It refers to inner peace. Jesus told His disciples, "Peace I leave with you; my peace I give you. I do not give to you as the world gives. Do not let your hearts be troubled and do not be afraid" (John 14:27). The world's peace is situational; it is based on outward circumstances. The peace that Christ offers is an inner peace that prevails regardless of circumstances.

Some years back in New York City, a famous art gallery sponsored a contest on the theme of peace. Several painters submitted works in the competition. The day of the judging arrived and the judges narrowed their choices down to two paintings. After lengthy deliberation, they made their final choice. The painting that came in second was a pastoral scene. It pictured a rolling green hillside with cattle peacefully grazing and puffy white clouds lazily floating across the sky.

A Hearty Greeting

The winning painting was a scene from the New England coast. It pictured a storm at full fury. The dark green waves smashed up against the giant rocks on the coast, thrusting foam and spray many feet into the air. The sky was an angry greenish black split by a bolt of lightning. Down in one corner of the picture was a seagull peacefully sitting on her eggs in a nest safely nestled in the cleft of a rock. The raging storm could not touch it. So it is when we have God's peace; the raging storms of life cannot touch us.

Christianity is not a magic wand designed to wisk us out of trouble, but a source of strength and power to see us through our problems. We, as Christians, are not exempt from the ravages of sin. We are subject to the same buffeting by life that is the lot of humankind. The difference is that the Lord is with us through the storms of life. Later in this epistle we will find that Paul was able to rejoice even in prison.

DISCUSSION QUESTIONS

1. Read Acts 16:11-40. Why do you think this was Paul's first stop in Europe?
2. Why is service from love more effective than service from duty?
3. Why do you think we emphasize the negative aspects of holiness rather than the positive aspects in many of our churches? What can we do to change this?
4. How did Paul and Silas evidence "grace and peace" in the Philippian prison? How can we evidence "grace and peace" in our trials?
5. Read Ephesians 2:8-10. What is the relationship between grace and service?

2

Expression of Love

PHILIPPIANS 1:3-11

*W*hen we think of great men and women of God, we often think of their prayer lives. How would you like to be able to listen in on the prayer life of Luther, Calvin or Wesley? What about Charles Finney, D.L. Moody or A.B. Simpson? What about Edith Schaeffer, Billy Graham or Charles Swindoll? We may not have the opportunity to share the prayer lives of these servants of God, but the apostle Paul has shared some of his prayer life with us through his epistles.

THANKSGIVING

In this letter to the church at Philippi, Paul follows his salutation with a recounting of his prayers for the believers in that church. He begins by telling how he thanks God for them (v. 3). In fact, in seven of his nine epistles written to churches, Paul reminds his readers in the first chapter that he thanks God for them. In this letter he tells the believers why he is thankful for them: "because of your partnership in the gospel from the first day until now" (v. 5).

Expression of Love

The word translated *partnership* (*fellowship* in the KJV and *participation* in the NASB) means a joint participation in a common interest or activity. The common interest or activity is the proclamation of the gospel. The preposition *in* used in this verse is a preposition of motion in Greek, hence the Philippian believers were participating in the proclamation of the gospel.

Some of the best fellowship I have experienced has been with those who have shared in ministry with me. When others and I are planning a ministry, praying for a ministry and working on that ministry, a closeness develops that I do not find in other situations; a comradeship in ministry that cannot be duplicated.

The fellowship of the saints in ministry should be a constant source of joy and thanksgiving for the believer. In America today we are developing a spectator mentality concerning the gospel. We come to church to be ministered to. We leave churches that "do not minister to us." We look to the professionals to minister. Then we wonder why there is no joy in our Christian life and why our fellowship seems so superficial.

God has created us to find meaning and purpose in His service. The joy of the Lord and the fellowship of the saints are found in ministry. This explains why Paul and Silas could sing in that Philippian jail. Many of us still believe that joy comes from receiving, when the Scriptures clearly teach that joy comes from giving and serving. When we give of ourselves in ministry with other believers, we find real joy and meaningful fellowship. Then we begin to understand the reason for Paul's thanksgiving.

ASSURANCE

Another aspect of the joy and fellowship we find in Christ is our assurance of salvation. If our salvation was based on works, as it is in many false religions and cults, our service for Christ would be motivated by duty and fear so there would be no joy. But because our salvation is based on faith in Jesus Christ, our service is motivated by gratitude and love which produces joy. Our assurance of salvation is a basis for fellowship and ministry.

In verse 6 Paul gives us the divine basis for assurance: "being confident of this, that he who began a good work in you will carry it on to completion until the day of Christ Jesus." What Paul basically said is that God finishes what He starts.

In baseball today the relief pitcher plays an increasingly significant role. Relief pitchers such as Rich Goosage, Rollie Fingers, Bruce Sutter and Ron Davis are as well known as the best starting pitchers. Most baseball managers are happy to have seven or eight good innings of pitching from a starter, then in come the bullpen aces.

God, however, does not need relief help from us. The death of Jesus Christ made full atonement for all our sins. There is nothing left to do. When Jesus was crucified, He said, "It is finished" (John 19:30). When Christ died, our salvation was made complete. Jesus was God incarnate, without sin. Being sinless, He did not need to die, but He took our sins and died for us. All that is left is for us to respond by faith.

Because our salvation is based on Jesus Christ and His atonement and not on our works, we can have assurance of salvation. Paul teaches the same truth in his second letter to Timothy where he writes: "I know whom I have believed, and am convinced that he is able to guard what I have entrusted to him for that day" (1:12). The apostle John writes, "And this is the testimony: God has given us eternal life, and this life is in his Son. . . . I write these things to you who believe in the name of the Son of God so that you may know that you have eternal life" (1 John 5:11, 13).

In addition to the divine assurance, Paul tells us in verse 7 about the human evidence of assurance. Paul was assured of the salvation of the saints at Philippi because of their behavior. Their works were evidence of their salvation.

Now wait a minute, you may be thinking, I thought you just wrote that salvation is by faith not works. You are absolutely correct. Works do not produce salvation; however, salvation does produce works. Listen to what Paul told the church at Ephesus: "For it is by grace you have been saved, through faith—and this not from yourselves, it is the gift of God—not by works, so that no one can boast. For we are God's workmanship, created in Christ Jesus to do good works, which God prepared in advance for us to do" (Ephesians 2:8-10).

James makes the same point in a different way when he writes: "As the body without the spirit is dead, so faith without deeds is dead" (James 2:26). The evidence that a body is alive is a pulse, breath and body temperature. The evidence that a person has spiritual life is good works.

If we are truly converted, there should be evidence of it in our lives. Because the false religions and cults have placed such an emphasis on good works, many of us have down played the importance of good works in the Christian life. There are a few verses in John's apocalypse that help us understand the place of good works from God's perspective: "Let us rejoice and be glad and give him glory! For the wedding of the Lamb has come, and his bride has made herself ready. Fine linen, bright and clean, was given her to wear (fine linen stands for the righteous acts of the saints)" (Revelation 19:7-8). The bride of Christ, of course, is the church. The bridal gown will be made of the righteous acts of the saints. How are we contributing to that garment?

LOVE

What is the greatest evidence that we have placed our faith in Christ? Jesus Himself tells us, "All men will know that you are my disciples if you love one another" (John 13:35). In Philippians 1:8, Paul tells the saints of his affection for them. Paul had a deep love for his brothers and sisters in the Lord. He demonstrated that love in his shepherding of the churches and his prayers for the saints. It is important in the church that we express our love for each other. Unexpressed love is love withheld.

Paul not only expresses his affection for the Philippian believers, he prays that their love might abound (9-11). There are five different Greek words that are all translated *pray* in our English Bibles. The word Paul uses here means to make a request with a definite aim. Paul's prayer in these verses is very specific.

While romantic love may be blind, or at least so the poets tell us, Christian love is open eyed and has a clear vision (v. 9). The word translated *knowledge* means to observe fully or to notice attentively. The word translated *depth of insight* (*judgment* KJV, *discernment* NASB) is only used in this verse. It is not found anywhere else in the Greek New Testament. The Greek words generally translated *judgment* or *discernment* have an emphasis on making a decision. The word used here, however, emphasizes perception or clear sight.

In verse 10 Paul tells us the purpose of this complete observation or clear insight: it is to be able to discern (*approve* KJV and NASB). This word, a banking term, means to test in the sense of checking to see if it is true or good. Coins were tested to see if they were genuine or counterfeit. What are we to discern? That which is best.

As we mature in our Christian walk, our choices are not between the good and the bad. We are able to see those things that are obviously wrong. Rather, our choices are often between the good and the best. The Greek word translated *discern* literally means, "to be better than." Why do we need to choose the best? So that we can be pure and blameless until we see Christ.

When Jesus was asked what was the greatest of all commandments, He replied, "Love the Lord your God with all your heart and with all your soul and with all your mind" (Matthew 22:37). He also said, "The second is like it: 'Love your neighbor as yourself'" (Matthew 22:39). Then He added, "All the Law and the Prophets hang on these two commandments" (v. 40). The apostle Paul also taught that all the commandments "are summed up in this one rule: 'Love your neighbor as yourself.'...Therefore love is the fulfillment of the law" (Romans 13:9-10).

When we love each other we not only fulfill the law, we demonstrate that we are Christ's disciples. It is interesting to note that the birth of Christ is not discussed in every New Testament book, neither is the death nor resurrection of Christ, nor the plan of salvation. But one thing that is discussed in every New Testament book, including the one-chapter books of Philemon, Second and Third John and Jude, is love between the brothers and sisters of Christ. Paul writing to the church at Corinth says, "And now these three remain: faith, hope and love. But the greatest of these is love" (1 Corinthians 13:13). If it were not in the Bible, we would consider it heresy for someone to say love was greater than faith. But Paul declares it so.

If the Christian church ever began to really understand and practice the biblical teaching on love, we would have a church-growth movement beyond imagination. There are millions of people in this world who would give anything for real love. If the church demonstrated real love, people would flock to us. That is why Jesus taught that people would know we were His disciples when we truly love each other.

Where does this kind of love come from? Paul tells us when he prays the saints will be "filled with the fruit of righteousness that comes through Jesus Christ" (v. 11). Most commentators see the fruit of righteousness as synonymous with the fruit of the Holy Spirit found in Galatians 5:22-23. Jesus Christ indwells every believer through the Holy Spirit (Romans 8:9-11; 1 Corinthians 13:12, 27). Love is the first fruit of the Holy Spirit. The apostle Paul tells us, "God has poured out his love into our hearts by the Holy Spirit" (Romans 5:5).

It is not easy to love each other in the Body of Christ. Like brothers and sisters in a human family, we get on each other's nerves. We annoy each other. We step on each other's toes. We differ in our views and convictions, tastes and desires. There are any number of reasons why we find it hard to love each other. Yet, if we allow the Holy Spirit to take control and produce His fruit in our lives, we can love each other.

One of the reasons we find it hard to love each other is that we do not understand *agape* love. In our culture, love is understood basically as an emotion. It involves feelings. We associate love with warm feelings and positive emotional experiences. We have romanticized love. Agape love, however, is not related to feelings. The heart, in both Hebrew and Greek cultures, was not the seat of the emotions. The bowels (the intestines, the abdomen) were the seat of the emotions. The heart, in those cultures, was the seat of the will. It was the place decisions were made.

The classic definition of agape love is found in 1 Corinthians 13:4-8. A careful reading of those attributes of love reveals an absence of emotions and feelings. Love is defined in terms of attitudes and actions. We can choose, with the help of the Holy Spirit, to have right attitudes and actions toward others, and when we do, the positive feelings will be there.

In these verses we have been looking at, Paul rejoices and is thankful for Christian fellowship. When we have fellowship centered around the ministry of the gospel, produce the works that evidence our salvation and love each other, our joy also will be full. Joy is one of the major themes of this epistle and in these verses Paul begins to let us in on the secret of joy.

DISCUSSION QUESTIONS

1. Read the following passages on Paul's prayers: Romans 1:8; 1 Corinthians 1:4-8; Ephesians 1:15-18; 3:14-19; Colossians 1:3; 1 Thessalonians 1:2-3; 2 Thessalonians 1:11-12. What common themes and concerns do you find? How do they compare with his prayer in Philippians? What applications can you make to your prayer life?
2. Read the following passages: Psalm 119:63; Acts 1:14; Romans 1:12; 16:1-16; Galatians 2:9; Colossians 2:1-5; 1 Thessalonians 5:11; Hebrews 10:24-25. How do these verses relate to Paul's discussion of fellowship in Philippians?
3. Why do you think God included love between the believers in every book of the New Testament? Why did Jesus say love was how people would know we were Christians, rather than faith, orthodoxy,

church attendance or holy living? Why did Paul
say love is greater than faith?
4. What is the relationship between faith and good
works? Why should a living faith produce good
works? What works?
5. What are some ways in which the good can keep us
from the best in our fellowship with other believers?

3

Situations and Somebodies

PHILIPPIANS 1:12-20

A re you an actor or a reactor? Do you react to circumstances and people, or do you act in a biblical manner regardless of them? Most, if not all, of our difficulties come from either situations or somebodies, that is, either circumstances or people. The apostle Paul was no different from the rest of us; he faced difficulties with circumstances and people. In this passage, we will see how Paul handled his difficulties and derive some principles we can apply to our situations and with our somebodies.

SITUATIONS

The story is told of a Chinese man who lived in feudal China when the warlords reigned. The man had one son and one horse. One day the son left the corral gate open and the horse ran away. The man's neighbors came by to say how bad it was that the horse had run away. The man replied, "How do you know it is bad?"

The next day the horse returned, leading 13 wild horses into the corral. The man's neighbors came by to say how good it was that he had 13 more horses. The man replied, "How do you know it is good?"

When the man's son went out to begin breaking one of the new horses, he fell off and broke his arm. Again the man's neighbors came by to say how bad it was that his son broke his arm. The man replied, "How do you know it is bad?"

The next day a Chinese warlord came by and took all the healthy boys off to war. The man's neighbors came by and said how good it was that his son had a broken arm and was not taken.

So often we allow our situations or circumstances to control us and our attitudes and feelings. We are like the Chinese man's neighbors, every turn of events controls us. Paul learned to handle his circumstances rather than let them handle him. Instead of bemoaning his imprisonment, Paul used it as opportunity to proclaim the gospel to his prison guards, which actually led to the spread of the gospel. In verse 12 we see that Paul practiced what he preached in Romans 8:28, "And we know that in all things God works for the good of those who love him, who have been called according to his purpose."

When we find ourselves in difficult circumstances, do we use them as an opportunity to share our faith or minister to others, or are we so busy feeling sorry for ourselves that we miss the opportunities God gives us? I read recently of a young boy who was in the hospital dying from cancer. Before he went to be with the Lord, he had shared his faith with several of the hospital staff caring for him. Some of them accepted his testimony and believed in the Lord.

Paul's behavior in difficult circumstances became a testimony and an inspiration to other believers (v.14). When the Christians of his day saw Paul was willing to

Situations and Somebodies

suffer for the sake of the gospel, it encouraged and challenged them to boldly speak the Word of God. When we are in trying and difficult circumstances, is our behavior an example and encouragement to other believers? Do we act in such a way that others gain courage from us? Do others forge on for Christ because of what they see us doing? This passage is a good reminder of an important truth: our behavior not only affects us, it also impacts the lives of others.

In both 1 Corinthians 11:1 and Philippians 3:17, Paul could say to the believers that they should follow his example. Each of us has others looking to us for an example. If we are a Sunday school teacher, youth sponsor, club leader, Bible study leader or involved in some other ministry, we have young Christians looking to us for an example. If we are parents, our children look to us for an example. Sometimes when I watch my son and daughter play "house" it is like watching a movie of my wife and myself. By the way Paul responded to adverse circumstances, he set an example for the other believers.

SOMEBODIES

Sometimes our problems and difficulites do not arise from circumstances, but from people. Paul tells his readers that there are some preaching the gospel, not out of concern for the lost, but from selfish ambition (vv. 15-18). These people were apparently envious of Paul's success and considered him their rival.

Who were these individuals, preaching from ambition, envy and jealousy with the purpose of causing Paul trouble? Some have suggested that they were Judaizers or false prophets seeking to undermine the message Paul preached. The text implies, however, that they were preaching the true gospel (v. 18). Back in

21

verse 14, Paul says, "most of the brothers." Then, in verse 15, he adds, "It is true that some preach Christ out of envy and rivalry. . . ." These also were brothers.

It is sad but true that some ministry is carried out from wrong motives. Some Christians minister from ambition, envy and rivalry. A few years back I was with a group of evangelical pastors from a local area. Someone suggested that the churches sponsor a community Easter sunrise service at a local shopping mall. The first reaction of some of those pastors was, "Who gets to preach?" and "Who gets the visitors?" Their primary concern was not with reaching the community but with protecting their "turf."

Apparently these people that Paul was writing about were orthodox Christians. Unfortunately, their main motivation for preaching the gospel was to build themselves up and show up Paul. They thought their success would irritate Paul and make him jealous.

Paul's action, however, was just the opposite of what those ministering from selfishness and envy expected. They expected Paul to react in anger, jealousy and discouragement, but he responded with rejoicing: "The important thing is that in every way, whether from false motives or true, Christ is preached" (v. 18).

This passage raises an important question: If the gospel is preached from impure motives, will it be effective? It seems that Paul believed so. The narrower question might be: Is the power in the message or the messenger? Ideally both. The gospel of Jesus Christ should be proclaimed by Spirit-filled men and women. But the gospel is true no matter who proclaims it or for what reasons. There is power in the message. The Bible is replete with examples of godless persons whom God used to proclaim His message. The classic Old Testament example is found in Numbers 22—25 where Balaam prophesied the Word of God.

In the Sermon on the Mount, Jesus spoke of people who had effective ministries but were not true believers.

> "Not everyone who says to me, 'Lord, Lord,' will enter the kingdom of heaven, but only he who does the will of my Father who is in heaven. Many will say to me on that day, 'Lord, Lord, did we not prophesy in your name, and in your name drive out demons and perform many miracles?' Then I will tell them plainly, 'I never knew you. Away from me, you evildoers!'"
>
> MATTHEW 7:21-23

When the gospel of Jesus Christ is proclaimed, the truth can impact people's hearts.

Frequently, our most serious difficulties and problems do not come from those outside the household of faith but from brothers and sisters in Christ. We tend to think that the world will oppose us and cause us problems. While this can be true, in American society the world is often only indifferent to us. We are not subject to persecution as many are in other parts of the world. In fact, "religion" is somewhat fashionable in our culture.

It is easy for petty jealousies and envy to creep into our relationships with other believers. So often we feel slighted. We need to be careful not to become offended over every little thing others do. Someone has said that the most difficult instrument to play in the church is second fiddle. We will be amazed at what we can accomplish if we are not concerned about who receives the credit.

On the other hand, we need to examine our own motives for ministry. Are we ministering out of envy, rivalry or selfish ambition? Does pride, prestige or power motivate us? We also need to be sure we are not the somebodies in other people's lives.

SOLUTION

We, like Paul, face difficulties with situations and somebodies. What is the solution to these problems? According to Paul, this solution takes two forms: "For I know that through your prayers and the help given by the Spirit of Jesus Christ, what has happened to me will turn out for my deliverance" (v. 19). Reading that verse carefully, we see that Paul is not referring to his own prayers, but to the prayers of others for him. Part of Paul's solution to situations and somebodies was to encourage people to pray for him.

In chapter 2, we looked at Paul's prayer life. We saw that in most of his epistles he recorded his prayers for the saints. He also recorded prayer requests in many of his epistles (e.g., Romans 15:30-32; Ephesians 6:19-20; Colossians 4:2-4; 1 Thessalonians 5:25; 2 Thessalonians 3:1-2). Paul was not afraid to share his fears, weaknesses and needs. He earnestly solicited the prayers of his brothers and sisters in Christ.

Paul believed in the power of prayer. Things happened in his life because others prayed. In the first chapter of Second Corinthians, Paul tells about many of the problems he faced and how God delivered him. "As you help us by your prayers," he writes, "then many will give thanks on our behalf for the gracious favor granted us in answer to the prayers of many" (v. 11).

Do we really believe this? Do we believe the prayers of our fellow Christians can help us? So often when we are facing difficulties from situations or somebodies we do everything but pray. We complain, we gossip, we nag, we act nasty—in a nutshell, we act unchristian. It is in times of difficulty that we need to turn to our brothers

Situations and Somebodies

and sisters in the Body of Christ.

When situations and somebodies overwhelm us, we need to take them to the Lord in prayer but not just by ourselves. We need to share our requests with other believers and have them pray with us and for us. American culture places a strong emphasis on independence and self-reliance. Christianity and the church, however, were meant to have Christians function interdependently. Scripture clearly teaches that the Body of Christ is interdependent (1 Corinthians 12:12-26). One of the major provisions for maintaining a Christian walk is prayer for one another.

In addition to prayer, the ministry of the Holy Spirit in our lives can enable us to deal with our situations and somebodies. The Spirit of Jesus Christ (v. 19) refers to the Holy Spirit (Galatians 4:6; Romans 8—9). Jesus Christ is present in every believer through the Holy Spirit. Like Paul, we need to look at the power of Christ in us, not at the power of things over us. Jesus said that all power had been given to Him and that He would be with us forever (Matthew 28:18-20).

The Holy Spirit produces love, joy, peace, patience, kindness, goodness, faithfulness, gentleness and self-control (Galatians 5:22-23). The Christian life is meant to be lived in the power of the Holy Spirit (Acts 1:8) as we walk in the Spirit (Galatians 5:16-26).

In dealing with situations and somebodies, we find Paul's expectation and hope (v. 20). It is his desire to do nothing of which he will be ashamed, but rather to have the courage to live, or die, so that Christ will be exalted. One reason why we have problems with circumstances and people is that we are concerned with ourselves. We will find that many of our so-called problems will disappear when we cease to be concerned about ourselves and become more concerned with the exaltation of Christ and the welfare of others.

Chuck Swindoll tells about a man with whom he was counseling. The man said, "Under these circumstances I would expect to feel bad." Chuck responded, "What are you doing under there?" We need to realize that many times we are not in a position to change circumstances and people, let alone control them. The one thing we do control, though, is our response to them. And this is often where the problem lies.

As we make it our aim to exalt Christ, we will begin to see our situations and somebodies not as problems but as opportunities. With the apostle Paul we will be able to rejoice over the opportunities that come into our lives.

DISCUSSION QUESTIONS

1. What are some of the situations or somebodies which give you problems? How can you apply the principles discussed in this chapter?
2. Why do some of our greatest difficulties come from other believers? What can we do about it?
3. Why do you think so many Christians do not ask for prayer when they are facing problems? How can we encourage them to do so?
4. Look up Romans 15:30-32; Ephesians 6:19-20; Colossians 4:2-4; 1 Thessalonians 5:25; 2 Thessalonians 3:1-2. What types of things did Paul ask prayer for?
5. Why is it that our reactions to situations and somebodies are generally the real source of our problems?

4

I Don't Want to Die

PHILIPPIANS 1:21-26

*I*n the passage we are considering in this chapter, Paul says he would rather die and be with Christ than stay here on earth. While doing research for this book, I visited the office of a New Testament professor at the Bible college where I teach. As we were discussing a particular textual problem, the professor said to me, "I look forward to asking Paul about that when I get to heaven." Then he paused and added, "But I hope I don't get the chance too soon." Like most of us, the professor was ready to die and even looked forward to heaven, but he wasn't interested in going quite yet.

Remember that Paul was writing this epistle from a Roman prison. He was facing the very real possibility of execution at any moment. Many Christians had already met their death and he could be next. Being in that situation changes one's perspective on life and death. Let us look at Paul's struggle with the question of life and death and how it applies to our lives today.

THE CHOICE

I read recently about an older woman who was flying to New York City. The airliner developed mechanical problems, and the passengers became quite upset. All except the older woman who remained quite calm. The passenger seated next to her asked how she could be so relaxed. The woman replied, "I have a husband who went to be with the Lord a few years ago and a daughter living in New York. I would be just as happy to see either one."

Paul is saying in these verses (21-22) that it would be great to go and be with the Lord, but he still had things to do here on earth. He expresses a similar sentiment in Second Corinthians 5:8 where he writes, "I . . . would prefer to be away from the body and at home with the Lord." He adds that it is his goal to please Christ in life or in death (v. 9).

A number of commentators suggest that when Paul writes, "For me . . . to die is gain," he is not speaking of personal gain. They point out that Paul has been speaking about the spread of the gospel and the exaltation of Christ (Philippians 1:12-26). If the spread of the gospel would be furthered by his death, then that would be gain. This is an interesting interpretation. It is certainly consistent with all we know about Paul. It seems to me, however, given the context, that Paul is saying he is ready to go home and would be overjoyed to be with Christ. Let us look at the options Paul faced.

DEATH

Paul was ready to die. The word *depart* is translated from a Greek word used to speak of untying a ship from its moorings or striking a tent. As a tentmaker, Paul was probably using it in the latter sense. In either case, the word has the connotation of beginning a journey. Paul saw death not as an end, but as a beginning.

Why was Paul ready to die? Because he knew that to be absent from the body was to be present with the Lord. Paul believed in the resurrection of the dead. He wrote to the church at Corinth, "Christ died for our sins according to the Scriptures, that he was buried, that he was raised on the third day according to the Scriptures. . . . Christ has indeed been raised from the dead, the firstfruits of those who have fallen asleep" (1 Corinthians 15:3-4, 20). Since Christ was resurrected from the dead, Paul believed all who would place their faith in Him for salvation would also be raised from the dead.

Thus Paul was able to face death confidently, even expectantly. We can also face death confidently, yes, even expectantly, if we have placed our faith in Jesus Christ as our personal Savior. The Bible teaches that God created us to be His children and serve Him. But we rebelled and decided to live our own way, to live for ourselves (Genesis 3:1-17; Isaiah 53:6; Romans 3:23). The result of our rebellion or sin is death (Romans 5:12; 6:23).

Thankfully, God in His love for us, sent His Son, Jesus Christ, to die in our place (John 3:16; Romans 5:18-19). When we are willing to confess our rebellion or sin and ask Jesus Christ to be our Savior, He comes to be with us through the Holy Spirit and gives us eternal life. While we still face physical death, God gives us spiritual life. When our earthly bodies, which have been contaminated by sin, finally die, God will give us resurrection bodies for eternity (1 Corinthians 15:35-41; 2 Corinthians 5:1).

Another thing we need to notice is that Paul had no

desire to die as an escape from this life (Philippians 1:21-26). His desire was to be with Christ. He was facing death at the hands of the Romans and saying, "If I am killed it will be gain, because I desire to be with Christ and death will bring that about."

The same is true for our loved ones who have died in the Lord. We need not grieve for them, rather we ought to rejoice for them as they are with Christ. It is true that we miss our loved ones who have died, but death is a temporary separation. As Christians we know there is the hope of a joyous reunion with our loved ones. We can find comfort in these verses when believers go to be with the Lord.

Paul was coming to the end of his life and facing execution. When God calls His children home, He prepares them. God gives dying grace to His saints. Paul's growing desire to be with Christ must be understood in light of his approaching homegoing. The word *desire* in the Greek means a passionate craving.

Perhaps our desire for heaven is not as great as Paul's because we have a wrong view of heaven. I will confess that for years after I was saved, I viewed heaven as a celestial retirement village. I figured that we would all sit around and occasionally attend a praise service. To be honest, the thought of heaven did not excite me. Sure, it was a lot better than the other option, but not very enticing.

While the Scriptures give us very little information about heaven, they do seem to indicate that it will be a place of activity. From what we know of the nature of God, it will be creative activity. As I have studied Scripture further, my earlier conceptions of heaven have changed. In a number of Jesus' parables about His return or Second Coming, He indicates that the reward for faithful service in this life will be even greater opportunities for service in the next life (e.g., Matthew 25:14-29; Luke 19:11-26). Not only will heaven be a place of activity and service, but there will not be any sin to thwart and frustrate us.

One of the more detailed descriptions of heaven is found in Revelation 22:1-5. This passage describes a beautiful garden city. A crystal clear river flows through its center, with the tree of life growing by its side. In verse 3 it says that the curse will be removed. But we want to notice the rest of the verse which reads, "The throne of God and of the Lamb will be in the city, and his servants will serve him." The word *servants* is the Greek word *doulos* that Paul used back in Philippians 1:1. It refers to Christ's disciples. What type of service will the servants of Christ render? Verse 5 tells us, "And they will reign for ever and ever." We will continue to serve our Lord in heaven.

LIFE

While Paul desired to be with Christ, he also had meaning and purpose in life. "It is more necessary for you that I remain in the body," he says (v. 24). Even while in prison and facing martyrdom, Paul's concern was for the needs of others rather than his own. If it were necessary, he would willingly remain on earth and continue to minister to the churches.

In verse 25, Paul says, "I know I will remain, and I will continue with all of you. . . ." Had Paul received a special revelation from God or had his legal situation taken a favorable turn? Neither. It was the needs of the churches that convinced him that it was not his time to go to be with Christ.

He further explains that he is remaining "for your [Phillippians'] progress and joy in the faith" (v. 25). The word translated *progress* originally referred to a pioneer blazing a trail through a new territory. The Christian life was not meant to be a static experience; it was meant to be a growing one. There are always new areas to move into. What is the result of this progress or growth in the faith? It is joy.

Our tendency, however, is to look for joy in all the wrong places. Some of us invest in homes, cars, clothes and other material possessions thinking they will bring us joy. Others of us strive for success and achievement believing they are the source of joy. It is true we may find momentary pleasure in these things, but never joy. Pleasure is based on circumstances. So when circumstances change, pleasure is gone. On the other hand, joy is based on an inner reality, the work of the Holy Spirit, and remains unaffected by circumstances.

Paul writes, "so that through my being with you again your joy in Christ Jesus will overflow on account of me" (v. 26). The word translated *boast* in Ephesians is the same word translated *joy* in Philippians 1:26. The New American Standard Bible probably best translates this verse by rendering it, "so that your proud confidence in me may abound in Christ Jesus through my coming to you again."

Their proud confidence or boasting was not in themselves or even in Paul but in Jesus Christ. Paul wrote to the Corinthians, "Let him who boasts, boast in the Lord" (1 Corinthians 1:31). We cannot boast in our works or our accomplishments, but we can boast in Christ Jesus and His works through us. As Paul wrote, "Therefore I will boast all the more gladly about my weaknesses, so that Christ's power may rest on me" (2 Corinthians 12:9).

Jesus Christ gives meaning to life and serving Him gives purpose to life. Life without Christ is merely existence, but He promised, "I have come that they

I Don't Want to Die

might have life and have it to the full" (John 10:10). The servant of God is immortal until his or her work is done. We need to be about His business.

Paul looked at the choice between life and death. It is a choice we must face, too. Are you ready to die? If you know Jesus Christ as your personal Savior, you can answer yes. Are you ready to live for Christ? He demands total allegiance and complete obedience; in exchange He gives real joy.

DISCUSSION QUESTIONS

1. Do you believe that as Christians approach their homegoing, their desire to be with the Lord increases? Why?
2. Read 1 Corinthians 15:3-8, 20-28, 35-39. Why is the resurrection of Christ central to our hope of eternal life?
3. What is your concept of heaven? How did you come to it? Read John 14:2; Luke 20:34-36; Acts 7:55; Hebrews 11:10, 16; Revelation 7:9-19; 21:1-27; 22:1-5. How do these passages affect your view of heaven?
4. What is the difference between pleasure and joy? Can a Christian experience joy in the midst of trials?

5

How to Be Unpopular

PHILIPPIANS 1:27-30

*E*veryone wants to be popular. Each of us wants to be liked and accepted by others. But what price are we willing to pay for popularity? Are we willing to compromise our lifestyles? Our principles? Are we willing to "go along to get along" even when it violates the clear teachings of God's Word? Or are we willing to risk being unpopular to remain faithful to our convictions?

Unfortunately, there are times when remaining faithful to our Christian convictions will result in unpopularity with the world. In these verses (1:27-30) Paul sees a cause and effect relationship. He sees Christian conduct as the cause and unpopularity, the effect.

THE CAUSE: CHRISTIAN CONDUCT

The word translated *conduct* in our English Bibles is the Greek word *politeuo* (v. 27). It refers to the public duties of a citizen. You will recall that when Octavius conquered the city, he awarded Philippi the *ius Italicum*, the "Italic right." The people of Philippi were well aware of the responsibilities of citizenship.

How to Be Unpopular

In the third chapter of this letter Paul reminds his readers that in addition to their earthly citizenship, they also have a heavenly citizenship (3:20). Even as there are responsibilities resulting from earthly citizenship, so there are responsibilities for the citizen of heaven. Paul says we should carry out the responsibilities of our heavenly citizenship in a manner worthy of the gospel. Paul insisted on the highest standards for the saints and taught that they should behave in a worthy manner (Romans 16:2; Ephesians 4:1; Colossians 1:10; 1 Thessalonians 2:12). Someone has asked the question: "If it were illegal to be a Christian and you were arrested, would there be enough evidence to convict you?"

What is the evidence of Christian citizenship? It is the unity of the saints. Jesus taught, "All men will know that you are my disciples if you love one another" (John 13:35). As He prayed for His followers, Jesus asked, "May they be brought to complete unity to let the world know that you sent me and have loved them even as you have loved me" (John 17:23). Two aspects exist to this unity (Philippians 1:27). The first is positional, "Stand firm in one spirit." Jesus said we are to love each other. Who is Jesus talking about? Those who agree with us on baptism? Those who are members of our church or our denomination? Those who believe the same as we do about the rapture? Those who follow the same lifestyle we do? No! It is those who are one in spirit with us. Those who have received Jesus Christ as their personal Lord and Savior. While our views on baptism, the rapture and other issues are important, they are not salvation or fellowship issues. The issue that is vital to spiritual unity is a personal relationship with Jesus Christ (1 John 4:1-3; 5:1-5).

The second aspect of unity is practical, "contending

as one man for the faith of the gospel" (v. 27). The word translated *man* (*mind* KJV, NASB) is the Greek word *psyche* from which we derive the word psychology. The context in which this Greek word is used determines its meaning in a given passage. But the central concept of psyche is "life-force." In our English New Testaments, it is translated life, soul, heart and mind. The NIV is alone in translating psyche as man (and only in this instance). As has been pointed out, the context determines the meaning. Out of a dozen versions, all but two translated psyche as mind or heart.

In this context, the concept clearly is mind (you will recall that for the Greeks the heart was the seat of the will). Paul is referring to the human will, to the center of moral decision-making. Although we need to be of one mind, Paul is not asking us to be of one mind on everything. He is very specific. We are to be of one mind on the "faith of the gospel." This is the word *evangelion* and means good news. What is the evangelion? Paul tells us, "I want to remind you of the gospel . . . that Christ died for our sins according to the Scriptures, that he was buried, that he was raised on the third day according to the Scriptures" (1 Corinthians 15:1, 3-4).

As one spirit, we are to contend for the gospel. A very interesting word for contend, *synathleo*, is used. It is actually made up of two words: *syn*, meaning with and *athleo* (from which we derive athletics) meaning a sporting event or competition. Paul is encouraging his readers to work together as an athletic team does to proclaim the gospel. Evangelism is not an individual event, it is a team sport. It will take cooperation to accomplish the Great Commission. The only way we can work together as a team is to be of one spirit and one mind.

The unity that we need can only be built on love for

each other, not a natural love, but a supernatural love. If Christ lives in us through the Holy Spirit, we have the power to love. As Paul wrote to the church at Rome, "God has poured out his love into our hearts by the Holy Spirit, whom he has given to us" (Romans 5:5). When all of us as Christians begin to work together as a team to proclaim the gospel, there will be consequences.

THE EFFECT: UNPOPULARITY

When we boldly proclaim the gospel of Jesus Christ, there will be those who will oppose us. But Paul exhorts us to contend for the faith "without being frightened in any way by those who oppose you" (v. 28). The apostle Peter writes, "Even if you should suffer for what is right, you are blessed. . . . 'Do not be frightened.' But in your hearts set apart Christ as Lord" (1 Peter 3:14-15). Both Peter and Paul echo the teaching of Jesus who taught that we should not fear those who are able only to do us physical harm (Matthew 10:26-28).

If we are living for Christ, we will be unpopular. Our lives will be a conviction to those around us. If we are not unpopular, perhaps we are too comfortable with the world and they are too comfortable with us. The world was not comfortable with Jesus Christ; in fact, they killed Him. Jesus told His followers:

> "This is my command: Love each other. If the world hates you, keep in mind that it hated me first. If you belonged to the world, it would love you as its own. As it is, you do not belong to the world, but I have chosen you out of the world. That is why the world hates you. Remember the words I spoke to you: 'No servant is greater than his master.' If they persecuted me, they will persecute you

also. . . . They will treat you this way because of
my name, for they do not know the One who sent
me."
JOHN 15:17-21

Here again we find the relationship between unity
and love within the body and opposition without. Because the world hates us and opposes us, we need each
other. We cannot let minor doctrinal differences and
religious practices divide true followers of Christ. We
must join together, "contending as one man for the
faith of the gospel."

In his second letter to Timothy, Paul writes, "In fact,
everyone who wants to live a godly life in Christ Jesus
will be persecuted" (2 Timothy 3:12). It is interesting
to note that Paul does not say may, might or could, he
says *will* be persecuted. Why are we not hated as Christians? Why are we not persecuted? Why do we not face
opposition? It is because we are not bothering anyone.
We are not challenging anything. We are not making
the world uncomfortable.

Christianity has always been a revolutionary force.
Even a casual reading of the Bible and world history
reveals that true Christianity has never been comfortable with the status quo. A.W. Tozer has said,

> We who preach the gospel must not think of our-
> selves as public relations agents sent to establish
> goodwill between Christ and the world. We must
> not imagine ourselves commissioned to make
> Christ acceptable to big business, the press, the
> world of sports or modern education. We are not
> diplomats but prophets, and our message is not
> compromise but ultimatum. (*Man: the Dwelling
> Place of God*, © 1966 Christian Publications,
> Camp Hill, PA.)

How to be Unpopular

A word of explanation should be offered here. We need to make sure that it is the gospel that is an offense and not ourselves (1 Corinthians 1:23). We must be kind, gracious and loving. The Scriptures command us to live at peace with everyone if at all possible (Romans 12:18). Too often we can be rude and obnoxious, and when we are opposed, we claim we are suffering for righteousness' sake. We represent a God whose very essence is love. We bring a message of hope, reconciliation and forgiveness. Our methods must be consistent with our message and our Lord.

While we are kind, gracious and loving, we also must be uncompromising. The question we all must ask ourselves is this: Am I willing to pay the price of discipleship? We should take our stand against sin. We should tactfully excuse ourselves when our co-workers begin telling dirty stories. Even if we did not say anything about their behavior, our actions would be convicting. What would happen if we refused to participate in dishonest business deals? What would happen if we did not allow our children to participate in questionable activities when our neighbors were allowing their children to take part?

When God's power is manifested in people's lives, there may be a cost. A good example of this is found in Mark's Gospel. Jesus and His disciples were crossing the Sea of Galilee on their way to the region of the Gerasenes. When they landed, a demon-possessed man came out of the tombs and approached them. The local people had tried to chain this man up and subdue him but were unable to do so. The man ran to Jesus and dropped to his knees before Him; he asked Jesus not to torture him.

When Jesus asked the demon his name, he replied, "Legion, for we are many" (5:9). They begged Jesus not to send them away, so He dispersed them into a large herd of pigs nearby. The pigs ran off a cliff into the lake and drowned. When the local population came out and discovered the man healed and their pigs dead, they were concerned about their pigs. Instead of welcoming Jesus who had just healed the man, they asked Him to leave because He had cost them their pigs (5:1-20). We think people will be impressed with what God offers them; however, people often only see the cost and are not interested.

All through the ages God's people have suffered for taking a stand for righteousness. David writes, "Those who repay my good with evil slander me when I seek what is good" (Psalm 38:20). Solomon warns us, "Bloodthirsty men hate a man of integrity" (Proverbs 29:10). The prophet Amos tells us that the wicked "despise him who tells the truth" (Amos 5:10). And then we have the words of Jesus, "Blessed are those who are persecuted because of righteousness, for theirs is the kingdom of heaven" (Matthew 5:10).

We have been given the privilege of suffering for Christ (Philippians 1:29). The word *granted* (*given*, KJV) means to give a gift or a special favor. This is a great source of comfort and encouragement for us when we suffer for Christ. When the world rejects us, we know that Christ accepts us. In trials, we have the opportunity to identify with Christ and share in His rejection by the world. This is not meant to create a martyr complex, rather it is to encourage us and help us endure.

In verse 30 Paul says, "You are going through the same struggle (*conflict*, KJV, NASB) you saw I had." The Greek word for struggle is *agon*, the root for *agony*. Paul is telling his readers that they are all in this struggle together. They are on the same team, contending for the faith of the gospel together.

How to be Unpopular

Even as Paul and the saints at Philippi struggled together for the gospel, so we must struggle together. We can no longer afford our factionalism as Christians. We need to put aside our petty differences and march forward together for Jesus Christ and His kingdom.

DISCUSSION QUESTIONS

1. What doctrines or issues do you believe are important enough that disagreement on them would preclude fellowship with other Christians? What is the basis for this?
2. Read 1 John 4:1-3, 7-13, 19-21; 5:15. What does John see as the basis for fellowship?
3. Read Romans 6:2; Ephesians 4:1; Colossians 1:10, and 1 Thessalonians 2:12. What do these verses have to say about living in a "worthy manner"?
4. Why do you believe Jesus taught love and unity were the best ways to reveal we are His disciples?
5. Have you ever experienced persecution for taking a stand for Christ? What were the issues?

6

Let's Get Our Act Together

PHILIPPIANS 2:1-11

*M*y wife has a plaque on the kitchen wall which reads, "I finally got it all together, and now don't remember where I put it." The expression "to get our act together" means to know what we are doing and how to go about it. For the servants of Jesus Christ, however, there is another sense in which we need to get our act together.

Jesus said, "All men will know that you are my disciples if you love one another" (John 13:35). He also asked His Heavenly Father "that all of them may be one," and, "May they be brought to complete unity" (John 17:21, 23). Not only do we need to get our act together as individuals, we need to act together as Christians. In these first eleven verses, Paul discusses Christian unity. This is not a theoretical discussion or the presentation of an ideal; rather, it is a practical discourse telling us what to do, how to do it and revealing the power to do it.

Let's Get Our Act Together

WHAT TO DO

In verse 1 in the NIV, the translators left out the key word *therefore* (see NASB, KJV). One of my former pastors would say, "When you see the word *therefore*, see what it is there for." Another pastor once said, "There is more blessing in the word *therefore* for the serious Bible student than almost any other word in the Bible." In most cases, therefore serves as a conjunction between what has been said and what is about to be said. Even more importantly, it tells us that what follows is a result of or conclusion from what preceded.

The word therefore in the first verse of chapter 2 is a bridge to carry us back to verse 27 of chapter 1, "Conduct yourselves in a manner worthy of the gospel of Jesus Christ." Using therefore, Paul is telling us that what he is writing in chapter 2 is how one lives in a worthy manner.

There is another key word in this first verse, *if*. In this context it is not used to indicate doubt or uncertainty; rather, Paul is using if in a rhetorical sense, indicating certainty without a doubt. He is asking a question that can only be answered by yes. Imagine you have bent over backward to be fair with another person, and she has not responded as you would have expected. You might say something like, "If I have been fair with you, shouldn't you be fair with me?" In this case you are not questioning your fairness, but rhetorically emphasizing it. This is the way Paul uses if in this verse. He is arguing that since we have received encouragement, love, fellowship, tenderness and compassion from Christ, we should so respond to other believers.

As we look at verses 1 and 2 in more detail, we will notice that they are parallel. While the New Testament was written in the Greek language, the authors were

Jewish. Maybe none was more Jewish than Paul, "circumcised on the eighth day, of the people of Israel, of the tribe of Benjamin, a Hebrew of Hebrews; in regard to the law, a Pharisee" (Philippians 3:5). Paul would have been very familiar with the Old Testament poetical books as well as other Jewish literature. Jewish poetry is unique. While the poetry of most languages, including English, is based on rhyme and meter, Jewish poetry is based on parallelism. That is, the same idea is repeated in different words. The rhyme is in the ideas rather than the sound. An example of this parallelism is Psalm 62:1:

> My soul finds rest in God alone;
>> my salvation comes from Him.
> He alone is my rock and my salvation;
>> he is my fortress, I will never be shaken.

Paul uses this Hebrew literary device in verses 1 and 2. The parallelism is presented below:

Verse 1 (Christ)	Verse 2 (Christian)
1. Encouragement	1. Being like-minded
2. Comfort from His love	2. Having the same love
3. Fellowship with the Spirit	3. Being one in spirit
4. Tenderness and compassion	4. Being one in purpose

Paul's argument is that what we have seen Christ do, we should do. First, Paul argues that if we have found encouragement in our union with Christ, we should encourage other believers by being united with them. Not necessarily united ecclesiastically or through ecumenical movements, but through like-mindedness. Paul writes in Romans 12:1-2 that God renews our minds. It is through the supernatural work of God that we can be like-minded.

Let's Get Our Act Together

Paul is not talking about being like-minded on baptism, or the Lord's Supper or the Second Coming. He is talking about being like-minded in the task of the gospel. When we share Christ's concern for the lost, that will transcend our petty denominational differences. We need to be like-minded, "contending as one man for the faith of the gospel" (Philippians 1:27).

Next Paul argues that if we are comforted by Christ's love for us, we should love each other. It is because Christ first loved us that we can love each other (1 John 4:10-11). We were loved when we did not deserve it. Since we have received love, we are able to love others even when they are not loving. Ironically, when others are the least loving, they need the most love. We conduct ourselves in a manner worthy of the gospel when we love one another.

Then Paul points out that we have fellowship with Christ through the Holy Spirit. Even as we have fellowship with the Spirit, we should be one in spirit. The Bible clearly teaches that every born-again Christian has the Holy Spirit (Romans 8:9-16; 1 Corinthians 6:19-20; 12:4-13). Therefore, if we are in fellowship with the Holy Spirit, how can we not be one in spirit with other believers?

Paul closes verse 1 talking about the tenderness and compassion of Christ. To be honest, there are many words we might use to describe the Christians we know, but rarely would compassion be one of them. Even as Christ has been tender and compassionate to us, we should be tender and compassionate to others. Compassion was a hallmark of Jesus' ministry (Matthew 9:36; 14:14; 15:32; 20:34; Mark 1:41; 5:19; 6:34; 8:2; 10:21; Luke 7:13; 10:33; 15:20). We need to be of one purpose, to show compassion to a world that needs Christ.

In a very straightforward way Paul has told us what

to do to get our act together: be one in spirit, be one in purpose, be like-minded and love one another. Now, how do we do that?

HOW TO DO IT

Again in verses 3 and 4, Paul uses the Hebrew literary device of parallelism. In each of these verses he first tells us not to be selfish, then he tells us to be humble. "Do nothing out of selfish ambition or vain conceit..." (v. 3). "Each of you should look not only to your own interests . . ." (v. 4). That is an excellent definition of selfishness, looking out for your own interests. Many people think hate is the opposite of love, but that is not true. Biblical love (*agape*) is selflessness, so the opposite of love is selfishness. Love puts others first, selfishness puts self first.

When my sister and I were children, an uncle placed a dime and a nickel on the table. I was older and knew the value of money, but my sister was too young to know a dime was worth more than a nickel. My uncle told her she could pick a coin—the idea being that if she were selfish and took the biggest coin, she would get less, but if she were selfless and took the smaller coin, she would get more. My sister took the larger nickel and left the smaller dime for me.

I cannot fault my sister, for too often in life I reach for what I believe will be best for me. Isn't that true for most of us? And yet, like my sister, we end up with less. We are so slow to learn that we cannot outgive God. When we give, we receive.

When we are selfish, we cannot be like-minded with other believers, because we think our views are best and right. The other person has to conform to our way of thinking. We cannot love others because selfishness is the opposite of love. We cannot be of one spirit with other believers. Selfishness keeps us from conducting ourselves in a manner worthy of the gospel.

On the other hand, humility enables us to consider others better than ourselves (v. 3). Paul says, ". . . but [look] also to the interests of others" (v. 4). Humility is not putting ourselves down, it is lifting others up. When we put others first, it is not hard to be of one spirit and purpose with them. The secret of unity is so simple and yet so difficult.

A person with great musical ability is asked to perform a special number in a worship service. If the person accepts the opportunity to perform in order to display his talents or show off, that is selfishness. The person is performing for his own benefit. If the person replies, "Oh, I can't do that, I'm not good enough," that is not true humility either. In fact, it may be a form of pride, seeking additional praise. True humility, however, recognizes one's God-given abilities and uses them for God's glory and the benefit of others. The humble person performs to minister—not for the sake of performing.

Most of us want to be humble, to put others first. Our problem is not in knowing what to do, it is in harnessing the power to do it.

THE POWER TO DO IT

Paul writes, "Your attitude should be the same as that of Christ Jesus" (2:5). What was His attitude? It was humility and obedience. Christ, the Son of God and God incarnate, became human (John 1:1, 14). As a servant, He gave His life. The idea of God partaking of humanity is beyond our comprehension. It is one of those things we accept by faith.

While Jesus Christ was fully human, He was also fully divine. Without giving up any of His divinity, He did give up the prerogatives of His divinity. The phrase "but made himself nothing" in verse 7 literally means to empty oneself.

God is omnipresent, yet when Christ took on humanity, He limited Himself to being in one place at a time. God is ominscient, yet Jesus said, "No one knows about that day or hour, not even the angels in heaven, nor the Son, but only the Father" (Matthew 24:36). God is omnipotent, yet Jesus was bound, beaten and crucified.

People often say that Jesus lived a sinless life because He was God. Yet He laid aside the privileges of His deity. In fact, the Scriptures teach that Jesus Christ performed His earthly ministry in the power of the Holy Spirit (Matthew 4:1; 12:28-32; Mark 1:12; Luke 4:1, 14, 18). The same Holy Spirit that indwelt Jesus Christ indwells us.

Jesus said to His disciples, "I tell you the truth, anyone who has faith in me will do what I have been doing. He will do even greater things than these" (John 14:12). How can we do the things He did and even greater things? Because we have the power of the Holy Spirit.

Since every true Christian has the Holy Spirit, the real question is, does the Holy Spirit have us? The Bible tells us we are to be filled with the Holy Spirit (Ephesians 5:18) and to walk in the Spirit (Galatians 5:25). God has given the Holy Spirit to each believer. The Holy Spirit convicts us when we do wrong and encourages us when we do right. We can choose to yield to the Holy Spirit or ignore Him. When we yield to Him and do as He prompts, He enables us.

In verses 9 to 11, we see the exaltation of Christ. Jesus Christ humbled Himself and became obedient to the Father; therefore, God exalted Him. These verses refer to the resurrection, ascension and glorification of Jesus Christ following His humiliating death. At the

end of this age, everyone, including those who crucified Him, will acknowledge Christ as Lord. The exaltation of Christ will be witnessed by all people. They will
recognize Christ as Lord by bowing the knee and con-
fessing He is Lord. When we are willing to be humble
and obedient, God will eventually exalt us.

Let's get our acts together as believers. In verse 2 Paul
says his joy would be complete if the saints at Philippi
would be like-minded, love one another and be one in
spirit and purpose. Paul has given us a very practical
formula for joy in the service of our Lord: strive for
fellowship and unity of the saints. The world teaches
pride and selfishness bring pleasure. Christ demonstrated that humility and obedience bring joy. When
we get our act together as the church of Jesus Christ, we
can know that joy.

DISCUSSION QUESTIONS

1. Read the second chapter of Proverbs. Each verse
   has two lines. Can you see the parallels between
   the first and second line in each verse?
2. How can we have unity between believers without
   ecclesiastical unity? Would a Billy Graham crusade
   be an example? Can you think of any others?
3. Read John 3:37-39; Romans 8:9-16; 1 Corinthians
   6:19-20; 12:4-13; 2 Corinthians 3:8; Galatians 4:6;
   Ephesians 1:17. What do these passages teach
   about believers and the Holy Spirit?
4. Read Matthew 9:36; 14:14; 15:32; 20:34; Mark 1:41;
   5:19; 6:34; 8:2; 9:22; 10:21; Luke 7:13; 10:33; 15:20.
   For what types of people did Jesus have compassion? What does that say about our purpose and
   ministry?
5. How do humility and obedience go together? Why
   does selfishness keep us from being obedient?

7

Faith and Works

PHILIPPIANS 2:12-18

*T*he highway between Jackson and Vicksburg, Mississippi, crosses several tributaries of the Mississippi River. One dark night, some years ago, a truck driver who was quite familiar with the road, was rolling along at 60 miles an hour. As he approached a bridge crossing one of the tributaries, the taillights of the car he was following dropped off into the darkness. The truck driver slammed on his brakes, but he was unable to bring his truck to a halt before it dropped into a black gap where a concrete span had once stood. His truck plunged into the river below. The driver was able to free himself and swim to shore before the truck sank. Dripping on the shore, he watched three more cars plunge into the river before he could get traffic stopped.

All of these drivers had faith that the bridge was there. Faith, however, is only as good as the object in which it is placed. Faith alone is not enough; it must have an object. I hear people say, "Just have faith" or "Only believe." But it makes a real difference what you have faith in. To have an object worthy of faith is not enough either; one must exercise faith in that object.

Several years ago I took flying lessons. After I had

mastered the basics, I began to learn to fly with instruments. I did a lot of flying "under the hood." The instructor would place a hood on my head that only allowed me to see the instruments. I could not see outside the plane. Once the instructor had me under the hood, he would do twists and turns to disorient me. He would then ask me to take over the controls and fly back to the airport by instruments.

One time on a cross-country flight we landed at the Altanta airport. When we were ready to fly out, visibility was below the limit for visual flight. We had to take off and fly by instruments. The Atlanta airport is quite busy with commercial jets constantly landing and taking off. In our small Cessna 172, a single engine, four-passenger plane, we had to have complete faith in the instruments and the air traffic controller. Our faith, however, was no good unless we obeyed the instruments and the controller. In fact, our obedience demonstrated our faith.

The passage we are considering in this chapter talks about the relationship between faith and works. This passage includes a verse that has given Bible students much trouble as well as some very practical truths for our lives. First we will look at the relationship between faith and works, and then we will look at the works of faith.

RELATIONSHIP BETWEEN FAITH AND WORKS

As we consider the relationship between faith and works, notice that verse 12 speaks of human responsibility while verse 13 speaks of divine enablement. Verse 12 begins with the word *therefore* (*wherefore*, KJV; *so then*, NASB). This connects us back to verse 27 in chapter 1, "Conduct yourselves in a manner worthy of the gospel of Christ." It is important that we see the context for this verse in order to correctly interpret it.

Paul addresses his readers as "my dear friends" (*beloved*, KJV, NASB). The Greek word is *agapectos*, from *agape*. The word literally means "loved one." Paul loved the brothers and sisters. Their obedience was an encouragement to him. Obedience demonstrates our faith in God and our love for Him. Jesus Christ taught, "Whomever has my commands and obeys them, he is the one who loves me" (John 14:21).

To a strong, faithful body of believers, Paul writes a phrase that has puzzled many and been a stumbling block to some: "Continue to work out your salvation with fear and trembling" (v. 12). Keeping the verse in its context, we know that Paul is writing to the saints about the work Christ has done in them (1:6). He is not teaching salvation by works because these believers were already saved.

If Paul was teaching salvation by works, it would contradict his other epistles. When the Philippian jailer asked, "What must I do to be saved?" Paul replied, "Believe in the Lord Jesus, and you will be saved" (Acts 16:30-31). Paul's message was always salvation by faith in Christ. To the church at Ephesus he wrote, "For it is by grace you have been saved, through faith...not by works, so that no one can boast" (2:8-9).

"Well, if it does not teach salvation by works, what does it teach?" you may ask. The Greek word translated "to work out" means to carry out or to complete a task. Earlier Paul wrote, "being confident of this, that he who began a good work in you will carry it on to completion until the day of Christ Jesus" (1:6). What Paul is discussing here is sanctification or living as a saved person.

But we do not have to work it out on our own; we have divine enablement. Paul writes, "For it is God who works in you to will and to act according to his good purpose" (2:13). God does not ask us to do what He does not enable us to do. The Greek word used for God working in us is *energein* and it means to energize or to empower. God empowers our will so that we choose to obey Him and He empowers us to do His will.

The Christian walk requires us to work out our salvation, that is, to conduct ourselves in a manner worthy of the gospel but with God's power and enablement. Most major religions, such as Islam, Hinduism and Buddhism, teach their followers to adhere to basic moral precepts. Each of these religions expect their followers to live according to the tenets of their faith. But one of the things that separates Christianity from these religions is that Christians are empowered by the Holy Spirit to maintain our moral standards and carry out the teachings of our faith.

WORKS OF FAITH

While salvation is by faith, saving faith produces works. After discussing salvation by faith and not works in Ephesians 2:8-9, Paul continues in verse 10, "For we are God's workmanship, created in Christ Jesus to do good works, which God prepared in advance for us to do." James writes, "Faith without deeds is dead" (2:26). Here in his letter to the Philippians, Paul goes on to look at some of the works of faith.

In verse 14, Paul says, "Do everything without complaining or arguing." Following a series of messages on the gifts of the Spirit, a woman came to her pastor and said, "I believe I have the gift of criticism." The pastor looked at her and said, "I have some biblical counsel on how to handle it." "What is that?" she asked. The pastor replied, "Do with your gift what the man who was given one talent did with it."

In our churches it is so easy to complain. The sermon is too long. The choir is too loud. The teenagers are too noisy. The ushers don't smile. On and on we can go. Complaining does not accomplish much, except to antagonize people. If there is something about your church that you believe needs to improve, work to make it better. If it cannot be changed, learn to live with it.

If anyone had a right to complain, it was Paul. When Paul came to Philippi, he was put into prison on false charges after having been beaten. No one could have criticized Paul for complaining. But he practiced what he preached. He and Silas sat in that jail rejoicing and singing praises. When we are serving God, situations that would normally lead to complaining become times of rejoicing.

When the teenagers are too noisy in church and someone complains, I say rejoice that they are here and not somewhere else. When young children run around at church functions and people complain, I say rejoice that our children are healthy and happy. If a guest speaker talks too long, be thankful that we have the freedom to gather and hear him. It is all a matter of perspective—almost anything that is a source of complaint is also a source of rejoicing.

In fact, if we were to carefully examine our complaints, we would find the vast majority result from selfishness. The sermon was too long because I had plans, not because the message was not needed. The children are too noisy because they bother me.

There is, however, a place for constructive criticism in the church. The distinction between constructive criticism and complaining is that complaining tends to tear down and discourage while constructive criticism tends to build up and encourage.

No one appreciates a contentious person. Like com-

Faith and Works

plaining, arguing is a matter of attitude. There is certainly a time and place to discuss the different sides of an issue, but the church's business, even our own business, should be conducted in love, free from anger and personal attack.

The church has a testimony to uphold before a watching world. Not only must we preach Christ, we must demonstrate that we are Christians, striving to be "blameless and pure, . . . without fault" (v. 15). Peter writes, "Live such good lives among the pagans that . . . they may see your good deeds and glorify God on the day he visits us" (1 Peter 2:12). If we live above reproach, we will stand out in a sinful world like shining stars in the midnight sky (Philippians 2:15).

Further admonishing the Philippian believers, Paul says "Hold out the word of life" lest my labor be in vain (v. 16). The word for "hold out" is the same Greek word used when a host offered a beverage to a guest. There is some question as to what Paul means by "the word of life." He may be referring to Jesus Christ. John calls Jesus the Word of life (1 John 1:1). It may also refer to the gospel, the message of life. Whether Paul is referring to Christ or the gospel of Christ is not an important distinction. What is important is that we be about the business of holding Christ out to the world through our testimony.

From their works of faith, Paul knew the Philippians were following the gospel. While only God knows who has genuine faith, He has taught that real faith produces works. If our lives do not demonstrate our faith, what do they demonstrate? A.W. Tozer, in *That Incredible Christian*, wrote that we will be known by:

What we want most
What we think about most
How we use our money
What we do with our leisure time
The company we enjoy
Whom and what we admire
What we laugh at

Few Christians are as fervent in their testimony as was Paul. In spite of his sufferings—imprisonments, chains, trials, shipwreck—his service produced joy (vv. 17, 18). A joy based not on circumstances, but on a relationship with God and obedience to His commands. For Christians, some moments of greatest joy can be found in the most adverse circumstances. Anyone can be happy and cheerful when life is going well, but the mark of a Christian is the ability to rejoice in any circumstance.

We have been saved by faith unto good works. Are we producing good works? Do people know we are Christians by our actions? Are we above reproach, holding forth the word of life? Does our life measure up to our message?

These are soul-searching questions. If we have answered them honestly, we may not like what we have discovered about ourselves. But finding out the truth about ourselves is the first step to change. Now we need to work out our salvation, to live worthy of the gospel. We need not, however, do it on our own. God works in us to enable us and empower us. Through the indwelling Holy Spirit, we can be all God would have us to be.

DISCUSSION QUESTIONS

1. How does obedience demonstrate love?
2. Why do you think there is so much complaining and

arguing in most churches? What are some things
you could do to help eliminate it in your church?

3. How can we distinguish between complaining and
    constructive criticism? What examples of each
    would illustrate this?

4. Can there be differences of opinion in a church
    without argument? How should they be handled?

5. Is it possible to have faith without works? Explain
    your answer.

8

The Preacher and the Layman

PHILIPPIANS 2:19-30

*I*n November of 1959 at Madison Square Garden, the champions of the National Horse Show were being presented. It was time for the champion jumper. The big gray horse entering the center ring was obviously not a thoroughbred. The crowd was silent as the spotlight followed him into the ring. Horse and owner then turned to face the crowd. Suddenly the arena erupted; thirteen thousand spectators were on their feet cheering.

Paul Harvey goes on to tell how this unlikely champion came to beat every other jumper in the show. It began with a young man named Harry de Leyer. He was raised on a farm in the Netherlands and married his childhood sweetheart. Together they traveled to America. Harry and his bride tried their hands at raising tobacco in North Carolina, working on a horse farm in Pennsylvania, and finally, he wound up as riding master at the Knox School for Girls on Long Island.

On a snowy Tuesday in February, Harry returned to

the school from the horse auction. When Harry opened the door of the horse van, out stepped a giant gray-white horse. The horse descended the ramp and stood in the snow. One of Harry's children, who had come out to see the new horse, remarked, "He looks just like a snowman."

The name stuck. Snow Man was easy to train and became a good riding horse. Harry and the horse developed a special relationship. As school closed for the summer, a neighbor offered Harry double what he had paid for Snow Man. While Harry had enjoyed Snow Man, he could not afford to be sentimental. After all, he was in business to make a profit.

That was when Snow Man revealed his real talent. Even though the neighbor had very high fences, Snow Man managed to jump them and return to Harry. After this happened several times, Harry bought Snow Man back. The rest is history. Snow Man won show after show culminating with the National Horse Show at Madison Square Garden and "Horse of the Year" honors two years in a row.

No one would have known of Snow Man's talents if it had not been for a neighbor's high fences and an auction on a snowy Tuesday in February, a few years earlier. Harry had arrived late at the auction that day; the best of the lot had already been sold. But when the giant gray gelding was brought out, Harry was able to look past the protruding ribs, the matted mane and the sore-scarred legs to an inner quality. Harry outbid the only other person interested in the gray giant—the buyer from the glue factory.

God loved us and saw potential in us even when we were scarred by sin. He paid a tremendous price for us, the life of His only begotten Son. Christ's sacrifice makes it possible for us to develop into productive

Christians.

After challenging his readers to imitate Christ, Paul closes this chapter with two examples of men who conducted themselves in a manner worthy of the gospel of Christ. One is a preacher, the other is a layman.

THE PREACHER

Timothy, a disciple of the apostle Paul, served as an itinerant preacher and as pastor of the church at Ephesus. He was probably led to Christ by Paul. The apostle speaks of Timothy as his spiritual son (1 Corinthians 4:17; 1 Timothy 1:2). Raised in a Christian home under the godly influence of his mother Eunice and his grandmother Lois (2 Timothy 1:5), Timothy entered Christian service at a young age and was respected (Acts 16:2). Following his call to the ministry, he was ordained (1 Timothy 1:18; 4:14; 2 Timothy 1:6) and accompanied Paul on his third missionary journey (Acts 17). The writer of Hebrews also tells us that Timothy spent time in prison as did his mentor (Hebrews 13:23).

In chapter 2, we see two things about Timothy. First, Timothy was concerned for the welfare of the saints (vv. 20-21). While others were looking out for their own interests, Timothy was concerned with Christ's interests. It is not just pastors who should be concerned with the welfare of the saints and the interests of Jesus Christ.

The Scriptures make it abundantly clear that we are to watch out for each other's welfare. We are taught to help restore our brothers and sisters when they fall into sin and to bear each other's burdens (Galatians 6:1-2). Believers are to build each other up in the faith (Ephesians 4:12), to pray for each other (Ephesians 6:18), to teach and admonish each other (Colossians 3:16), to encourage each other to love and good deeds (Hebrews

10:24). The apostle Paul wrote to the church at Rome that the saints should be devoted to each other and give preference to each other (Romans 12:10).

The second thing Paul says about Timothy, in verses 22 to 24, is that he is of proven worth. That is, he was living worthy of the gospel of Jesus Christ. Timothy was living up to the faith Paul had placed in him. He demonstrated his worth by his life. Jesus Christ has put His faith in each one of us. Are we living up to that faith?

Someone might argue that Timothy was a preacher, not an appropriate example to hold up to laymen. Pastors are expected to be good and live right. Let me say, as a pastor, that ministers are only sinners saved by grace. We face the same temptations and problems that other Christians encounter. Even though this objection lacked validity, Paul may have anticipated it, so he also included an example of a layman.

THE LAYMAN

The name Epaphroditus means lovely or charming. It is an apt description of this man's Christian walk. Epaphroditus is only mentioned in Philippians (2:25; 4:18). He was a layman in the church at Philippi, possibly a deacon or in some other position of lay leadership. How does Paul feel about Epaphroditus?

First, Paul called Epaphroditus a brother (v. 25). While all Christians are brothers and sisters in the Lord, Paul is emphasizing the special bond that had developed between them. Several years ago, I ministered in a migrant farm camp with another young man. During that year of ministry, we grew especially close. We prayed together, worked together, laughed together and cried together. Our relationship became very special. I have had very deep relationships with men I have ministered with on church staffs. While every believer is my brother or sister in the Lord, the concept takes on a deeper meaning for those with whom I minister.

Secondly, Paul did work closely with Epaphroditus. As a "fellow worker," Epaphroditus pulled his load. He was faithful to the task. The church needs men and women who are willing to work and serve our Lord.

Thirdly, Paul calls him "fellow soldier." Paul often used military metaphors to describe Christian life and ministry (Ephesians 6:10-17; 1 Timothy 6:12; 2 Timothy 2:3-4). He saw the believer involved in a spiritual warfare. Here was a man Paul could rely on in the heat of the battle of life. Epaphroditus fought well. He resisted Satan and stood firm for the Lord. We should strive to be people that others can rely on when the going gets tough.

Finally, Paul recognizes Epaphroditus as a messenger "whom you sent to take care of my needs" (v. 25). The NASB and the KJV say "to minister to my needs." The Greek word for minister used here is *litourges*, from which we derive *liturgy*. It literally means "service for God." This service to Paul was a spiritual ministry as opposed to physical ministry. While the Philippian church did send a financial gift by the hand of Epaphroditus (4:10-14), they apparently sent him primarily to minister to Paul spiritually.

When we think of the apostle Paul, we think of him ministering to others. It may be difficult for us to think of him needing to be ministered to. Yet here was a layman ministering to the apostle. What was true for the apostle Paul is also true for pastors. Because a pastor is always ministering to others, we may not think of his need for ministry. Even when we are aware of a pastor's needs, we often feel inadequate to minister to him. We think, "What can a layperson do for a pastor?"

The Preacher and the Layman

All believers, lay and pastoral, are to minister to each other. I am encouraged when a person tells me he or she has been praying for me. I am even more encouraged when someone asks if I have specific prayer requests. Pastors have the same needs and weaknesses as lay people, and we respond to the same types of ministry lay people need. Like Epaphroditus, we should minister to those in spiritual leadership. As believers, we are a "holy priesthood, . . . acceptable to God through Jesus Christ"; therefore, the pastor and the layperson are the same before God (1 Peter 2:4-10).

Epaphroditus was not only dear to Paul, he was loved by the Philippian church. He missed his church and longed to return to them and assure them he was all right (v. 26). Too often we become so concerned with our own problems that we fail to see the concerns of others. Here was Epaphroditus so sick that he almost died (2:27), yet he was concerned about others. I believe one of Satan's most effective tools for discouraging and immobilizing Christians is self-pity. We focus on ourselves and our problems and feel sorry for ourselves. One of the best cures for self-pity is to look to the needs of others and minister to them.

Men like Epaphroditus are to be honored (vv. 28-30). It is so easy to criticize the elders or deacons or second-guess the governing board. It is easy to find fault with the decisions of the trustees or question the wisdom of the Christian education committee. But the Bible instructs us to honor our spiritual leaders (1 Timothy 3:13; 5:17).

If a problem arises with someone in a place of spiritual leadership, pray about it. If it still bothers you, go talk to that person. Do not complain to others about it; do not even talk to others about it. Go directly to the person involved.

When persons in my congregation come to me with a complaint about one of the pastors on our staff or one of our lay leaders, the first thing I ask them is have they talked to that person yet. If they have not, I tell them that they should talk directly to the person and only come to me if the problem is not resolved. If they have talked to the person, I ask if we can have him or her present. We need to honor those in spiritual leadership and give them the benefit of the doubt.

Timothy and Epaphroditus are examples of men who lived worthy of the gospel of Jesus Christ. The challenge to us is to also live worthy of the gospel of Jesus Christ. The word *Christian* literally means "little Christs." Let us live up to our name.

DISCUSSION QUESTIONS

1. What are some specific ways you could minister to your pastor?
2. Read 1 Peter 2:4-10; Ephesians 5:19; Colossians 3:16; 1 Thessalonians 5:14-15; Hebrews 10:24. These passages are written to lay people. What do they say about the ministry of the laity?
3. Why is concern for the welfare of other Christians an important part of our walk with the Lord?
4. In verse 28, Paul says that the believers in Philippi would be glad when Epaphroditus returned and, in verse 29, Paul says they should welcome Epaphroditus with great joy. Why do you think people anticipated gladness and joy at this reunion? What does this say about our fellowship?
5. Why should we honor those in positions of spiritual leadership? What are some specific ways you could honor those in spiritual leadership in your church?

9

The Plan of Salvation

PHILIPPIANS 3:1-10

*S*holem Asch closes his great novel, *The Apostle*, in a Roman dungeon. Hundreds of Christians have been lowered through a little trapdoor into the dungeon. The awful knowledge that they will either die in the dungeon or be removed to die in the arena haunts them. Asch describes a scene of darkness and horror. Suddenly a shaft of light shines into the dungeon as the trapdoor is opened and a man is lowered down into the pit. As this man descends into this hole of darkness and despair, songs of praise and thanksgiving come from his lips.

Like wildfire the word spreads to the farthest corners of the dungeon, "It's Paul! It's Paul! Paul has come!" Before long the dungeon is filled with songs of praise and thanksgiving as Paul's joy spreads throughout the dungeon. Paul found joy in his Savior not his circumstances.

SERVING WITH JOY

NOT BY RITUAL

"Watch out for those dogs, those men who do evil, those mutilators of the flesh" (3:2). Who is Paul referring to with such strong language? He is referring to the Judaizers.

The Judaizers were Jews who accepted Jesus as Messiah but taught that faith in Christ was not sufficient for salvation. One also had to practice Jewish rituals and, in particular, circumcision. We first encounter the Judaizers in Antioch, "Some men came down from Judea to Antioch and were teaching the brothers: 'Unless you are circumcised according to the custom taught by Moses, you cannot be saved'" (Acts 15:1).

Paul and Barnabas challenged this teaching and went to Jerusalem to meet with the apostles and the elders to clear up the matter. At the meeting, "some of the believers who belonged to the party of the Pharisees stood up and said, 'The Gentiles must be circumcised and required to obey the law of Moses'" (Acts 15:5). Peter's response was, "No! We believe it is through the grace of our Lord Jesus that we are saved, just as they are" (Acts 15:11). And so the Jerusalem Council repudiated the teaching of the Judaizers and confirmed Paul's message of salvation by faith (Acts 15:12-21).

The Judaizers, however, were not satisfied. They continued to follow Paul and teach that one also had to be circumcised and follow the law of Moses to be saved. They followed Paul to Galatia and created an uproar in the church there. The whole Galatian epistle is a repudiation of the teachings of the Judaizers. They followed Paul to Corinth, and he had to warn the church in his second letter to them (11:13-15). Now they had apparently followed Paul to Philippi, and he was warning these saints about this false teaching.

The Plan of Salvation

While in Paul's day the Judaizers were teaching a salvation of faith plus works, there are those in our day who are teaching the same doctrine. Some groups teach that baptism is necessary for salvation. Now it is true that Jesus Christ commanded baptism (Matthew 28:19) and that baptism is an ordinance of the church, but baptism is not necessary for salvation.

There are groups that teach that church membership is necessary for salvation. Again, I believe church membership is important. Christians should become members of the church both as a display of identification and support and to fully participate in all aspects of church life including decision making. Church membership, however, is neither a prerequisite to nor a requirement for salvation.

Religious rituals result from our salvation; they do not provide salvation. Baptism and the Lord's Supper are testimonies of our faith, reminders of our salvation. The church ordinances are important and meaningful, but they are not the way of salvation. They are symbols of the way.

One reason it is so important for us to clearly understand the plan of salvation is so that we will not be led astray by false teaching. There seems to be something in most of us that finds legalism tempting. The idea of doing something to gain God's favor appeals to us. Rules and laws and rituals attract us. A complete understanding of the gospel is our defense against these false teachers and the appeal of their message.

NOT BY BIRTH

It is the policy of the church I pastor to only conduct weddings for believers. Any couple desiring to be married in our church must have an interview with one of our pastors and then go through premarital counseling.

I frequently have couples come in to inquire about a wedding. I explain to them our wedding policy and ask them about their faith. It is not uncommon for a person to claim he is a Christian because his parents are church members. Many people believe they are Christians because they were born into a "Christian home."

In verses 4 and 5, Paul argues that if salvation were by birth, he would have the best claim. He says that he was born an Israelite, one of God's chosen people, of the seed of Abraham and a part of the people of the covenant. Then he goes on to say that not only is he an Israelite, but he was from the tribe of Benjamin. The tribe of Benjamin had several claims to fame. The city of Jerusalem was within its territory. It remained loyal to Judah during the division of the kingdom of Israel. It was the tribe that was to lead Israel in battle (Judges 5:14; Hosea 5:8). Paul also claims to be a "Hebrew of Hebrews" (v. 5). This may refer to Paul's Jewish parentage. He may have claimed a pure lineage. It may also have been a reference to his being raised to speak Hebrew. Many of the Jews living outside of Palestine raised their children to speak Greek (they were called Hellenistic Jews). Paul goes on to say that he was raised as an orthodox Jew to be a Pharisee.

If salvation came by birth, then Paul had as much claim as anyone and more than most. But salvation does not come by birth. God does not have any spiritual grandchildren. Salvation cannot be passed on from parent to child. Each person must come to Christ on his or her own. While having Christian parents and being raised in a Christian home is a heritage one would wish for every child, a parent's faith cannot suffice for a child.

The Plan of Salvation

NOT BY WORKS

In the Old Testament, we find an interesting story about a captain in the Syrian army named Naaman (2 Kings 5). He was a great soldier and had led Syria to victory in its battle with Israel. Naaman, however, suffered from leprosy. In Naaman's home was a young Israelite girl who had been captured and brought to Syria as a household slave. This girl told Naaman's wife that there was a prophet of God in Israel who could cure Naaman. When Naaman heard about this, he went to the king of Syria. The king sent a letter with Naaman to the king of Israel asking for his healing.

When Naaman presented the letter to the king of Israel, the king was upset and thought the Syrians were looking for an excuse to go to war. But Elisha the prophet heard what happened and sent his servant to the king. He told the king to send Naaman to Elisha. When Naaman arrived at Elisha's house, the prophet did not even go out to see him. Rather, he sent his servant to tell Naaman to wash in the Jordan seven times. Naaman was furious. He said, "I thought that he would surely come out to me and stand and call on the name of the Lord his God, wave his hand over the spot and cure me of my leprosy" (2 Kings 5:11).

Naaman's servants went to him and said, "My father, if the prophet had told you to do some great thing, would you not have done it? How much more then, when he tells you, 'Wash and be cleansed'?" (2 Kings 5:13). How most of us resemble Naaman. We want to do some great thing to be saved, but all God says is to believe in His Son and be cleansed.

Back in Philippians, Paul says that if works could save, he would be first (3:6). He says he was zealous, legalistically righteous, in fact, faultless. Paul was as good as a human could be, but it was not good enough. Good works cannot save. The Scriptures make it clear that salvation cannot be obtained by works (Acts 13:39; Romans 3:28; Ephesians 2:9; Titus 3:5).

There are groups that teach that faith in Christ is not sufficient for salvation; good works are also necessary. This is especially true of cults. If we have real faith, it will produce good works. As Christians, we should be a people of good works. Good works, however, are to be a result of our salvation, not the means of our salvation (Ephesians 2:8-10). We are to demonstrate our salvation by our good works, but we cannot earn our salvation with our good works.

BUT BY FAITH

If salvation does not come by religious rituals, birth or good works, how is one saved? Paul writes that his circumcision, his birth and his good works are worthless, for salvation comes by faith in Christ (3:9). Jesus Christ died for our sins, and we must accept Him as our personal Savior by faith. There is nothing we can add to the work of Christ. He has done it all. The only thing left for us to do is come by faith.

While salvation is free, to be accepted by faith, discipleship is costly as Paul points out in verse 10. As followers of Christ, we join in "the fellowship of suffering" (v. 10). Paul raised the subject of suffering for Christ back in the first chapter, "For it has been granted to you on behalf of Christ not only to believe on him, but also to suffer for him" (1:29). There is a price to be paid in taking our stand for Christ.

On the other hand, Paul tells us of the power available to us for sharing the suffering. It is the resurrection power—a power that allows us to endure in suffering, even to rejoice. It is in suffering that we see resurrection power in action. When He was on earth, Jesus asked His disciples to give up all they had to follow Him (Matthew 10:39; Luke 14:33). Does Jesus ask any less of His disciples today?

All one has to do is visit any high school, college or professional football practice session to see athletes who are willing to suffer in order to compete. I have a son who plays high school sports. I have seen him play when he was so sore he could hardly move. Athletes are willing to suffer to win a sporting event. How much more should we as Christians be willing to suffer for Christ and His kingdom?

There are at least three applications we can draw from these 10 verses. First, if you are trusting in your baptism, church membership or other religious ritual for your salvation, place your faith in Jesus Christ. If you are trusting in the faith of your parents, place your faith in Jesus Christ. If you are trusting in your good works, place your faith in Jesus Christ.

Second, if you have accepted Jesus Christ as your Savior, share your faith with others. The plan of salvation was not meant to be a secret. It was meant to be shared. People cannot respond until they hear it (Romans 10:14). Even as the little Israelite girl shared the good news that there was a prophet in Israel, we need to share the good news that God loves the world and offers salvation freely to all who believe (John 3:16).

Third, the plan of salvation, when applied in our lives, should result in discipleship. We are to take up the cause of Christ, no matter the cost. Jesus Christ came not just to be our Savior, but also to be our Lord. We are called to discipleship. It is as we give up the things we think are valuable that we gain the things that are of eternal value.

DISCUSSION QUESTIONS

1. Read Galatians 3:1-14. What does this passage teach about the relationship between the law, faith and salvation?
2. Why do you think so many people find legalism appealing?
3. What is the relationship between faith and good works in the Christian life?
4. What are some ways in which we may suffer for the sake of the gospel in our culture?
5. Why is discipleship costly? Read Matthew 10:32-39; Luke 14:26-33; John 21:15-19.

10

The Purpose of Salvation

PHILIPPIANS 3:11-21

I recently read about an American oil company that was searching for a person to head its operations in Japan. The company became aware of a missionary in Japan who had an engineering degree. He also spoke fluent Japanese. He seemed to have the perfect background for the job. The oil company sent a high-level executive to Japan to recruit the missionary.

As they talked, the oil company executive told the missionary of their great plans for the Japanese market. He told the missionary of the benefits of working for his company. Then he offered the job to the missionary with a six-figure salary. The missionary turned the job down. The oil company executive was flabbergasted; he asked if the salary was insufficient. The missionary replied, "The salary is more than generous, but the job is too small." When someone has been in God's service, there are no other jobs to compare with it.

In the first ten verses of this chapter, Paul discussed the plan of salvation. Now he goes on to explain the purpose of salvation. God has a plan for His children.

Like the missionary in Japan, we have a calling. What the world has to offer us is not big enough; the challenge is not great enough. Paul tells us in these verses that we have eternal life, that we are in God's service and that we have a heavenly citizenship.

ETERNAL LIFE

There is much interest these days in life after death. There have been several books and articles describing people's claims to have returned from the dead and their descriptions of life after death. These reports are often contradictory and not always consistent with Scripture. But the Bible does tell us there is life after death.

All humans will have eternal existence. For those who have placed their faith in Jesus Christ as their personal Savior, it is called eternal life (John 10:27-28). They will spend eternity with God. For those who do not accept Jesus Christ as their Savior, it is called eternal death. They will spend eternity separated from God in hell. The Bible calls this the second death (Revelation 21:6-8).

When the Bible speaks of eternal life, it refers to more than eternal existence. Every human will go into eternity. Eternal life refers to a quality of existence. Eternal separation from God is like eternal death while being in God's presence will be life to its fullest. It will be life as God meant it to be when He first created humans.

Here, in verse 11, Paul refers to the resurrection of the dead. There is a word interjected into this verse that some may find troubling; it is the word *somehow*. Paul writes, "and so, somehow, to attain to the resurrection from the dead." It sounds as if Paul is not really certain about the resurrection. Paul's uncertainty, however, is not about the resurrection, but about how he will participate in it. Paul was looking for the imminent return of Christ. He also knew that death could come at any moment from the Romans. He was uncertain how he would be transformed, but he was fully confident that he would be transformed.

Nowhere does Paul more fully express his certainty in the resurrection than in First Corinthians 15. He says that the proof of our resurrection is Christ's resurrection. Paul argues that if Christ were not resurrected, then we have no hope of resurrection and are fools.

> But Christ has indeed been raised from the dead, the first fruits of those who have fallen asleep. For since death came through a man, the resurrection of the dead comes also through a man. For as in Adam all die, so in Christ all will be made alive.
>
> 1 CORINTHIANS 15:20-22

Paul certainly believed in the resurrection. He had no doubts about his eternal destiny. All of us who have placed our faith in Christ also have the sure hope of the resurrection. It is a great joy and comfort to know that we will spend eternity with our Lord. But Christianity is more than "pie in the sky by and by." We have been saved for a purpose, here and now. We have been saved to serve.

SERVICE TO GOD

Service to God gives life purpose and meaning. That's easy for you to say as a pastor and Bible college professor, you may be thinking. But what about me as a housewife, assembly-line worker or in the business world? For those who are heavily enmeshed in the work-a-day world, there are two possibilities. First, God may have something better for you if you are willing to be open to Him and step out by faith.

When I taught at Moody Bible Institute as well as at St. Paul Bible College, there were many students who were married, had families and were settled in a career. These men and women had felt God's call on their lives. They gave up careers, sold homes and came to Bible school to prepare for ministry. Some of them are on the mission field, others are in pastorates, but all are in a special place of service.

A couple in our church, in their forties with teenage children, gave up their home and careers and went with Wycliffe Bible Translators. He was a manager, she was an executive secretary. They are now using those skills in the service of the Lord. There are Christian ministries that need virtually every skill. I believe that a Christian should periodically reevaluate his or her life and make himself available for full-time Christian service.

While every believer needs to make himself available for whatever God has for him, I recognize that for many, God's place for them is where they are. That leads us to the second possibility, that God may have a place of service for you where you are. Most lay people have contacts with individuals whom pastors and evangelists will never have the opportunity to meet. We need to look at our place of work as a mission field. We also can look for opportunities for service in our local church. Some of the most significant ministries in the church are carried on by lay people. The Sunday school teachers have more opportunities to lead people to Christ than I do as pastor. It was a Sunday school teacher who led D.L. Moody to Christ.

Let us look at Philippians in more detail and see what Paul has to say to us about service. In 3:12, Paul says, "not that I have already obtained all this...." Obtained what? He is not referring to the resurrection, but is looking back to verse 10 and the power of the resurrection and the fellowship of suffering. Paul says he has not yet become all that he could be.

He continues in verse 12, "or have already been made perfect." The word *perfect* here does not mean sinlessness. Rather, it means spiritual fullness or maturity. Then Paul concludes in verse 12, "but I press on to take hold of that for which Christ Jesus took hold of me." What Paul is saying in this verse is that he has not yet arrived. But it is his goal to become all that Christ wants him to be. What about us? Is that our goal?

In order to be all that Christ intends us to be, we must forget the past and push toward the goal. We so easily become encumbered by our past sins and failures or we thrive on past achievements. We cannot let yesterday's failures fetter us or yesterday's successes carry us. Paul knew that the only hope of achieving the goal was to move ahead.

Are you allowing the past to control the present? If there is a sin that is holding you back, confess it, make it right and move ahead. Are you resting on yesterday's victories? Move on. Each day has new battles, new enemies to be conquered.

Long-distance runners know the agony of pressing toward the goal when they speak of "the wall." In a long-distance race, runners come to a point where they believe they can go no farther. They feel they have nothing left. They are sure they cannot take another step. At this point, the champion runners just put one foot in front of the other by sheer determination. They are running on "guts." But as they break through the wall, they get a second wind. They are able to go on and complete the race.

Each of us, in our spiritual lives, comes up to the wall. We feel that we cannot go on. There is nothing left. It is at those times we must continue by sheer determination. As we do, the Holy Spirit empowers us and enables us to carry on. When the going gets rough, we need to press on.

Remember, Paul is not writing this from a pastor's study or seminary office. He is sitting in a Roman prison facing a painful death. He has been betrayed by so-called friends. There are those who are ministering just to spite him (Philippians 1:15). Paul is not an armchair theologian. He writes from the harsh reality of life.

In verse 15, Paul writes, "All of us who are mature (*perfect*, KJV, NASB) should take such a view of things." Hey, wait a minute preacher, you may be thinking. Back in verse 12, Paul says he is not already perfect or mature and here in verse 15 he says he is. This sounds like a contradiction. In verse 12 Paul uses the verb form of *to be perfect*. In verse 15 he uses the noun form. Those who have a level of spiritual maturity recognize that they have not arrived. The more mature a Christian becomes, the more one recognizes how much farther he has to go.

Then Paul continues in verse 15 by pointing out that if anyone sees things differently, God will make it clear to him. Every believer is indwelt by the Holy Spirit. That means that God is present in each one of us. If we are open to His leading, He will lead us into the truth (John 14:16-17, 26; 1 John 2:20-21). Paul did not feel a need to argue his point. He simply stated the truth and then depended on God the Holy Spirit to convince his readers.

But we have made it this far, so let us keep going. Paul is telling his readers that they have attained a level of maturity. He wants them to live up to that—to live worthy of the gospel of Jesus Christ. He wants them to become all that Jesus Christ intends them to be.

The Purpose of Salvation

HEAVENLY CITIZENSHIP

In the closing verses of chapter 3, Paul discusses their heavenly citizenship. The Philippians could easily identify with the concept of citizenship because Philippi, as we noted earlier, had received the *ius Italicum*, the "Italic right."

Paul encourages his readers to follow his example and that of others who were living according to the Word of God (v. 17). Each of us is an example to someone. If we are parents, we are examples to our children. If we are Sunday school teachers, we are examples to our students. If we are in any leadership position in the church, we are an example. Someone is watching each one of us. The question is not, Are we an example? The question is, What kind of example are we? Can other believers follow us confidently? Let us commit ourselves to be the kind of examples that Paul speaks of in this verse.

Unfortunately, there are enemies of God's kingdom (vv. 18-19). These enemies are not outside the church but are found within the fellowship. Jesus spoke of them as the wheat and tares growing up together (Matthew 13:24-30). They claim to follow Christ, but, in fact, follow their own desires. Even today there are those who see Christianity as a means of health, wealth and prosperity.

Paul teaches, however, that Christianity involves service. We are citizens of heaven (vv. 20-21). Our goals and desires should not be earthly but heavenly. Our success is not to be measured in material terms, but spiritual terms. The prize we strive for is not found in this life, but the next. Paul looks forward to the resurrection and his transformation when he will be like Jesus.

As Christians, our allegiance is to another world. Remember what the missionary told the executive from the oil company, "Your job is too small." We are about the King's business. We are His ambassadors (2 Corinthians 5:20). Let us live worthy of our King.

DISCUSSION QUESTIONS

1. While some are called into "full-time" Christian service, what are some ways we can serve God right where we are?
2. What are some evidences of spiritual maturity? What are some things a person can do to continue to mature? What are some of the "walls" we come up to in our spiritual race?
3. Read 1 Thessalonians 1:7; 2 Thessalonians 3:7; 1 Timothy 1:16; 4:12; Titus 2:7; James 5:10; 1 Peter 5:3. What do these passages say about being examples?
4. Why do you think there is so much interest in life after death? Read Revelation 20:11—21:8. What do these verses say about life after death?
5. Read 1 Corinthians 15:1-7. Why was Paul so convinced of the truth of the resurrection?

11

We Are Being Watched

PHILIPPIANS 4:1-9

*P*eople are known by their behavior and attitudes. I taught an advanced psychology course at St. Paul Bible College called Personality Theories. While there are many different definitions of personality, most psychologists view personality as the source of consistency in a person's behavior across situations. It is this consistency that allows us to say, "Isn't that just like him." Or, "You would expect that from her."

People in the Bible were known for different things. David was known for his music and poetry. Peter was known for his impetuousness. Thomas was known for his doubting. Timothy was known for his timidity. Paul was known for his zeal for the lost. John was known as the apostle of love.

We can think of people we know in our churches. Some are known for their cheerful attitude; others are known for their complaining. Some are known as peacemakers; others are known as troublemakers. Some are known for their kindness; others are known for their selfishness. We as Christians are known for what we do, are and think.

In these opening verses of the fourth chapter, Paul talks about what Christians should do, be and think. Certain behaviors and attitudes will identify us as Christians. This is practical instruction for walking in a manner worthy of the gospel.

CHRISTIANS ARE KNOWN BY WHAT THEY DO

Paul begins with what to do. Obviously, we cannot know his motives for starting with behavior. Perhaps it was because he knew that what we do shapes who we are and what we think. Many people think that what a person is and what a person thinks controls his or her behavior. To some extent that is true, but modern psychological research has clearly demonstrated that our behavior controls our attitudes much more than our attitudes control our behavior.

Or, maybe Paul knew that what we do communicates more than what we say. We are all familiar with expressions such as, "What you are doing speaks so loudly, I can't hear what you are saying," or, "Actions speak louder than words." Paul discusses three areas of behavior that demonstrate our faith.

The first is, "Stand firm in the Lord" (4:1). Verse 1 begins with the word *therefore*. As we have already seen, the word *therefore* is used to connect us back to something that has already been said. At the end of chapter 3, Paul warned about false believers in the church. There are always those who want to compromise the message of the gospel, but we must stand firm.

Now, I feel compelled to give a warning at this point. It is in the gospel that Paul tells us to stand firm. It is not in our traditions or methods. Too often we confuse our message with our traditions and methods. Our message never changes, but our methods must constantly be under review.

When I was being interviewed for the pastorate of my present church, I told the people that there were two arguments I would never accept if I came as pastor. They were, "We've always done it this way," or "We've never done it this way." We have not been called to build traditions. We have been called to build a kingdom. Let us stand firm in the Lord, let us stand firm in the gospel, let us be uncompromising in our message, but let us be ready to use any means to proclaim that message.

The second area of behavior that demonstrates our faith is living in harmony with each other (vv. 2-3). Jesus taught, "Love one another. As I have loved you, so you must love one another. All men will know that you are my disciples if you love one another" (John 13:34-35). The apostle John wrote, "This is how we know who the children of God are. . . . Anyone who does not do what is right is not a child of God; neither is anyone who does not love his brother. This is the message you heard from the beginning: We should love one another" (1 John 3:10-11).

That all sounds great, you may say, but how do we handle conflicts in the church when they arise? Paul discusses a conflict between Euodia and Syntyche. Jesus Christ gave step-by-step instructions, recorded in Matthew 18:15-17, on how to handle the conflicts within the church. The first step is to go directly to the brother or sister who has offended us. We are not to go to the pastor, to our neighbor or to our friends, but to the person who has offended us. To discuss it with anyone else is gossip and divisive. If the other person listens to us and either agrees or gives a satisfactory explanation, we have won a friend without involving anyone else.

If the person will not listen to us or does not agree with us, then, and only then, we should tell it to two or three reliable, mature Christians who can maintain a confidence. Then we and these two or three others should go and talk with the person who has offended us. The reason for taking two or three others along is to have objective witnesses. It may turn out that we are wrong and the person we think offended us is right. Others can help discern the true situation.

If the witnesses agree with us, and the other person will not listen to them, then it should be told to the church. Now what does it mean to tell the matter to the church? There is honest disagreement among theologians and pastors as to how to apply this. Some teach that it should be presented to the whole congregation. Others argue that it should be brought to the leadership of the church. It is my feeling that it should be brought to the church's spiritual leaders. Different churches have different names for these persons. In our church it would be the Board of Elders.

There are several reasons why I feel this is best. First, it minimizes the number of people involved. Second, it prevents gossip. Third, it keeps the matter out of the hands of carnal Christians and non-Christians who may be present in the congregation. Fourth, and most important, the matter will be dealt with by mature Christians.

Jesus gives further instruction on handling conflicts in verses 21 to 35 of chapter 18 of Matthew. There He teaches we are to forgive each other. He tells a parable of a servant with a great debt who was forgiven by his master, but the servant would not forgive another servant who owed him a minor debt. God has forgiven us of all our sins; how much more we should be able to forgive those who offend us.

We Are Being Watched

Paul gives some additional counsel on handling conflicts in First Corinthians. In the sixth chapter he says that if we bring the matter to the church and the other person will not make it right, do not pursue it any further. Paul says in verse 7 that we should bear the wrong. He says that we are not to use the secular courts. It is hard to bear a wrong. There is something within us that cries to get even. That is where love comes into play. The way we love and forgive each other will be the clearest demonstration of our faith.

The third thing Christians do to demonstrate their faith is, "Rejoice in the Lord always" (4:4). Christians should be known as a joyful people. This does not mean walking around with a silly grin on our faces or laughing in times of tragedy. It is not irresponsible or unrealistic behavior. Rather, it is an attitude, a sense of contentment and peace. Real joy comes from the assurance that God is at work in everything.

It is easy for you to talk about joy, you may be thinking, but you don't know my situation. True, but I do know Paul's. He was in prison facing a death penalty. For those prisoners on death row today, we look for the most painless way to execute them. In fact, we use lethal injections in some states. But the Romans looked for the most painful and horrible means of execution for their prisoners. This is what Paul faced. He was physically ill and betrayed by his so-called friends. Yet, he was able to rejoice.

The command is not to rejoice in our situations but to rejoice in the Lord. Even non-Christians can rejoice when things go their way. More than just a positive mental attitude, true joy is supernatural. This joy is produced in us by the Holy Spirit and demonstrates our faith (Galatians 5:22).

CHRISTIANS ARE KNOWN BY WHAT THEY ARE

The first thing that Paul says Christians should be is gentle (*moderate* KJV, *forbearing* NASB). He says, "Let your gentleness be evident to all" (4:5). The word gentle has the concept of being satisfied with less than one's due, or sweet reasonableness.

In our country we have many "rights" movements. People are always concerned about their rights. I believe we as Christians should respect the rights of others, but should we go around demanding our rights? Are we willing to be slighted? Christ was gentle. He demanded nothing. "When they hurled their insults at him, he did not retaliate; when he suffered he made no threats" (1 Peter 2:23). As His followers, we should also be gentle.

A recent research project on anxiety found that 40 percent of the people studied worried about things that never happened. Another 30 percent worried about things over which they had no control, while 12 percent were found to have worries that were totally groundless. It is estimated that 50 percent of our hospital beds are filled with people who are suffering from psychosomatic ailments. That is, their illness was not caused by a virus, infection or accident but resulted from anxiety. Worry takes a great toll on our physical, emotional and spiritual being. Paul says we should not be anxious (4:6). Most human emotions are attributed to God: joy (Matthew 25:21, 23; Luke 15:7; John 17:13), anger (Deuteronomy 32:21; Hebrews 3:17) and grief (Genesis 6:6; Ephesians 4:30). But the Bible never tells us that God worries.

Paul counsels us, "In everything, by prayer and petition, with thanksgiving, present your requests to God" (4:6). Jesus taught, "Come to me, all you who are weary and burdened, and I will give you rest. Take my yoke upon you and learn from me, for I am gentle and humble in heart, and you will find rest for your souls" (Matthew 11:28-30). God is ready to take our cares, worries and frustrations. We need to bring them to God and leave them there.

This brings us to the third thing Christians should be—thankful (4:6). When we bring our requests to God, we should, by faith, thank Him in advance. A few days ago my son came to me and said he needed some money to go on a youth retreat. I told him I would work something out. He thanked me and went on his way. He did not ask me for details; he did not question me. He trusted me and knew I would work things out. Would our Heavenly Father do any less? Should we as His children do any less?

Finally, Paul writes that we should be peaceful (4:7). He tells us that the peace of God will keep our hearts and minds. What is the source of this peace? It is Christ Jesus. Jesus promises His followers, "Peace I leave with you; my peace I give you" (John 14:27). This is not a promise of peaceful circumstances. Around us there will be wars, quarrels, fighting and turmoil. But in the middle of this chaos we can have peace. God's peace is not based on circumstances, it is an inner peace produced by the Holy Spirit. As we turn our concerns and worries over to God and thank Him for His love and care, we will begin to experience His peace.

CHRISTIANS ARE KNOWN BY WHAT THEY THINK

Someone has said that 5 percent of the people in America think. Another 5 percent think they think. And the other 90 percent would rather die than think. Actually, that is not true. Everyone is always thinking. You even think when you are asleep. The question is, What do we think about? Another person has said, You are what you eat. To some extent that is certainly true. But even more true is the statement, You are what you think.

We think about what we put into our minds. Our children, in turn, will think about what we allow them to put into their minds. If we put good, wholesome thoughts into our minds, if we put biblical truth into our minds, that is what we will think about. If we put garbage into our minds, that is what we will think about.

People who feed on television, best-selling novels, the theater or any of our modern media indiscriminately, will find their minds reeling with sex, violence, hatred, murder and all forms of corruption. I am not saying all television, or all theater, or all best sellers are bad. But we do have to be careful about what we allow to enter our minds and our children's minds. My wife and I closely monitor the television in our home. We also explain to our children why we do not watch certain programs.

On the other hand, there are so many good wholesome thoughts to fill our minds. Obviously, first and foremost is the Word of God. There is also good children's literature. If you have not exposed your children to C.S. Lewis's *Chronicles of Narnia*, be sure to buy them. There is good music and art. There is the amazing world of nature. So much is good, positive and uplifting that we can expose ourselves to, there is little excuse for filling our minds with rubbish.

PUT IT INTO PRACTICE

Paul concludes this passage with a bold declaration: "Whatever you have learned or received or heard from me, or seen in me—put into practice" (4:9). Learning and practice go together. Christians are not to learn for the sake of knowledge, but for the sake of practice. We are to take the things we learn and apply them in our lives. Paul has told what Christians are to do, what they are to be and what they are to think. Now we need to put it into practice because the world is watching.

DISCUSSION QUESTIONS

1. How can we distinguish between our methods and our message? Can you think of examples of changing our methods without changing our message?
2. Do you think our behavior controls our attitudes more than our attitudes control our behavior? Why? Can you think of examples from your life or others you know that illustrate this?
3. Read Romans 12:19-21 and 1 Corinthians 6:1-8. What do these verses teach about demanding our rights?
4. What are some sources of garbage that we feed our minds on other than those mentioned? What are some additional sources of wholesome food for the mind?
5. What is one thing you learned from Philippians 4:1-9 that you can put into practice in your life this week? How will you do it?

12

The Contented Christian

PHILIPPIANS 4:10-13

*W*hen I first received my driver's license I did not have a car. I would have settled for any car. In fact, I did. I bought a 1948 Mercury Coupe from a farmer who had used it to haul manure around his farm. Before I bought that car, I believed that I would be happy with any car. But within a few weeks, I was looking enviously at my classmates with newer and nicer cars. I became dissatisfied with my old "junker." I believed that if I could get a newer car, I would be satisfied.

The next year I was able to buy a 1955 Chevrolet convertible. I was really happy with that car—for a while. I had some friends who had graduated from high school, were working full-time and had brand-new cars. So I thought a new car would bring satisfaction. A few years later, I bought my first new car, an inexpensive import. But within a few weeks, I was looking at fancier cars and wishing I had one.

How often life is like that. The next promotion, the next house, the new furniture. Just around the corner—that is where we think happiness and contentment are

to be found. Unfortunately, it is not true. A Greek phi-
losopher once wrote, "To whom little is not enough,
nothing is enough." If we cannot be satisfied with what
we have, we will not be satisfied with anything. In
verses 10-13, Paul tells us the secret of contentment.

CHRISTIAN CONTENTMENT

"I rejoice greatly in the Lord ..." (v.10). This is the key
to contentment. Paul does not rejoice in material possessions, position, circumstances or opportunities. He
rejoices in the Lord. How does Paul do it?

In verse 10 he refers to a gift that the Philippians had
sent him. He has already referred to their gift twice (1:5;
2:25-30), but he refers to it again because he deeply appreciates their generosity. Paul is not so much interested in the monetary value of their gift as he is in their
expressed concern for him. It is this that Paul really
appreciates. He points out that they had been without
opportunity to express their concern in the past, but
when the opportunity presented itself, they took advan-
tage of it.

We need to look for opportunities to express our concern for the spiritual leaders in our lives. What about
the faithful pastor who ministers in your church. Do
you take opportunity to show concern for him? Does
the congregation show concern for him? I am blessed to
serve a congregation where the people pay me a very
adequate salary. They show their concern for me and
my family in many ways. People are often dropping off
food, offering to perform services, giving us gifts and
in many other ways showing their concern.

In verses 11 and 12, Paul says that he is not bringing
this up because he has needs. He is saying, "I am not
looking for your gifts, I am looking for your concern. I
can be content under any circumstances. I have learned

to handle lean times as well as times of plenty." The key word is *learned*. He uses it in both verses 11 and 12. Contentment does not come naturally. Our natural tendency is toward selfishness. We want more and more; we are never satisfied. Dissatisfaction with what we have and the constant desire for more comes naturally. Contentment is learned.

To Timothy, Paul writes:

> But godliness with contentment is great gain. For we brought nothing into the world, and we can take nothing out of it. But if we have food and clothing, we will be content with that.
>
> 1 TIMOTHY 6:6-8

Paul says that we cannot take any of our possessions, positions or prestige with us. As Chuck Swindoll has said, "I have never seen a hearse pulling a U-Haul trailer." No matter what we amass here on earth, it will remain here. Therefore, Paul says, if you have enough to eat and something to wear, be content.

A VIEW FROM THE OTHER SIDE

The secret to learning contentment is learning to see things from God's perspective. We view things in terms of time; He views them in terms of eternity. We view things in terms of our desires; He views things in terms of His plan. We view things in terms of an earthly value system; He views things in terms of an eternal value system. We view things in terms of self-gratification; He views things in terms of service. How do we learn to see things from God's perspective?

First, we need to learn that we have been called to be servants. We are here to serve God, not please ourselves. Now one of the interesting things about Christianity is that the less we think of ourselves and the more we con-

The Contented Christian

centrate on serving God, the more joy we experience. The paradox is that the more we concentrate on our wants, the more dissatisfied we become; while the more we concentrate on serving God, the more content we become.

Second, we need to learn not to buy into the world's value system. The world judges us by the clothes we wear, the house we live in and the car we drive. The world looks at how much we get; God looks at how much we give. The kingdom values are laid out in the Sermon on the Mount:

> Blessed are the poor in spirit,
>   for theirs is the kingdom of heaven.
> Blessed are those who mourn,
>   for they will be comforted.
> Blessed are the meek,
>   for they will inherit the earth.
> Blessed are those who hunger and thirst for
>   righteousness, for they will be filled.
> Blessed are the merciful,
>   for they will be shown mercy.
> Blessed are the pure in heart,
>   for they will see God.
> Blessed are the peacemakers,
>   for they will be called the Sons of God.
> Blessed are those who are persecuted because of
>   righteousness,
>   for theirs is the kingdom of heaven.
>
> MATTHEW 5:3-10

These are certainly contrary to the world's values, yet the word *blessed* is in the plural in Greek and literally means *happinesses*. The word is used in Greek poetry to describe the joy of the gods.

Third, we need to learn that God loves us and cares

for us and watches over us. Jesus taught:

> "Therefore I tell you, do not worry about your life,
> what you will eat or drink; or about your body,
> what you will wear. Is not life more important
> than food, and the body more important than
> clothes? Look at the birds of the air; they do not
> sow or reap or store away in barns, and yet your
> heavenly Father feeds them. Are you not much
> more valuable than they? Who of you by worrying
> can add a single hour to his life?
>
> "And why do you worry about clothes? See how
> the lilies of the field grow. They do not labor or
> spin. Yet I tell you that not even Solomon in all his
> splendor was dressed like one of these. If that is
> how God clothes the grass of the field, which is
> here today and tomorrow is thrown into the fire,
> will he not much more clothe you, O you of little
> faith? So do not worry, saying, 'What shall we
> eat?' or 'What shall we drink?' or 'What shall we
> wear?' For the pagans run after all these things,
> and your heavenly Father knows that you need
> them. But seek first his kingdom and his right-
> eousness, and all these things will be given to you
> as well."
>
> MATTHEW 6:25-33

We need to learn that joy and contentment do not
come from things, but from God. When we learn this
lesson, we can say with Paul that we are content in any
circumstances.

POWER OF POSITIVE THINKING

In the past generation, Norman Vincent Peale made
a name for himself with a book entitled, *The Power of*

The Contented Christian

Positive Thinking. In our day, Robert Schuller, author of the best-selling book *Tough Times Never Last, But Tough People Do,* has made a name for himself with what he calls possibility thinking.

On a natural level, does possibility thinking work? It is a tough question to answer. We know, for example, that college graduates earn more money in a lifetime than high school graduates. But does the education make a difference? Would people who are smart enough to get into college and have the perseverence to stick it out succeed anyway? The same question can be asked about positive thinking. Do people who succeed think positively, or do people who think positively succeed?

Some recent psychological studies shed light on this question. In one study, two groups of people were given a series of mathematical problems to solve. Both groups were given the same problems and both groups did equally well. One group, however, was told they had done quite well; the other group was told they had done quite poorly.

Both groups were then given another series of identical mathematical problems. The group that was told they had done well on the first series did well on the second series. The group that was told they did poorly on the first series actually did do poorly on the second series. The group that thought they could do well did better than the group that thought they could not do well, even though both groups had demonstrated equal ability.

In medicine, we see the powerful effect of placebos. My wife is a nurse and worked for a while in a nursing home. The doctors would often order placebos for the patients. When a patient would complain about pain or insomnia or some other malady, he or she would be given a pill with no active ingredients. The patient would often show remarkable improvement because he or she believed the medication was working.

Evidently positive thinking does affect our actions and responses. For the Christian, however, the question is not, Does it work?, but What does the Bible say about it? The Bible has a great deal to say about thinking and our thought life. Proverbs 23:7 reads, "For as he thinks within himself, so he is" (NASB). Jesus said, "For out of the heart come evil thoughts, murder, adultery, sexual immorality, theft, false testimony, slander" (Matthew 15:19). Romans 12:2 reads, "Do not conform any longer to the pattern of this world, but be transformed by the renewing of your mind. Then you will be able to test and approve what God's will is—his good, pleasing and perfect will." Then, of course, there is Philippians 4:8, which we looked at in the last chapter: "Finally, brothers, whatever is true, whatever is noble, whatever is right, whatever is pure, whatever is lovely, whatever is admirable—if anything is excellent or praiseworthy—think about such things."

THE RIGHT MINDSET

Possibly the greatest example of positive thinking in all human history is found in Philippians 4:13, "I can do everything through him who gives me strength." Paul says "I can." There is a world of difference between saying I can and I can't. I can't admits defeat while I can claims victory. Here is Paul in prison, betrayed by so-called friends, all outward circumstances are against him, yet he says, "I can." The basis of Paul's positive thinking is not psychology; it is Jesus Christ. The key concept is "through Christ." I can't is the beginning of failure. I can is the first step of faith.

A recent Garfield the Cat cartoon showed Odie the dog chasing Garfield around the yard. Garfield heads for a tree and races up it. Odie races right up after him. As the two of them are resting side by side on a branch, their owner, Jon, comes by. He looks up at them and says, "Odie, dogs can't climb trees." The last frame shows Garfield thinking, "It's amazing what one can accomplish when one doesn't know what one can do."

It is so easy for us to stifle ourselves with negatives. In the church there is no place for negative thinking. On committees and boards I will not allow people to use arguments such as "We've never done it that way before," or "It won't work" or "We tried it once." There may be valid reasons why something should not be attempted, but negative thinking is not one.

On the other hand, positive thinking can turn what appears to be negative circumstances into positive ones. An elderly widow suffering from arthritis was confined to a nursing home. She had a room at the front of the building where she could watch the traffic go by. She said, "Isn't it good of God to let me have a room where I can watch the traffic." Some time later she was moved to a room in the back of the building. "Isn't this great of God," she said, "I can see the children playing in the back yards." Still later there was a move to the end of the building where her window faced the blank brick wall of the next building. "This is just great," she exclaimed, "I can look up and have a beautiful view of the sky." Here was a woman who had learned to be content in any circumstance.

We can't change what other people do. We may not be able to change our circumstances. But the one thing that is completely within our control is our reaction to them. Do we react negatively or positively? Do we see problems as disabilities or opportunities?

For the Christian, positive thinking is more than practical psychology; it is supernatural enablement.

It is through the power of Christ that we can learn to be content in any circumstance. Contentment and positive thinking go hand in hand because we have Christ indwelling us. As we see our circumstances from Christ's perspective, we will be content and know the joy of the Lord.

DISCUSSION QUESTIONS

1. Why do you think so many people are never satisfied with what they have? How does this affect Christians?
2. What are some areas in which an earthly value system conflicts with a godly value system?
3. What are some ways we can show concern for our spiritual leaders?
4. What are some ways in which Christians can practice positive biblical thinking?
5. It is not circumstances but our reaction to circumstances that affects our feelings. Can you think of a situation where your negative reaction to circumstances led to dissatisfaction? How might positive reaction have changed your feelings?

13

Whose Money Is It?

PHILIPPIANS 4:14-23

*W*ell, here we go again! I knew it. Sooner or later all you preachers get around to money. Maybe salvation is free, but the church surely is not. Money, money, money! It seems the church is always trying to get its hand into my pocket.

Why do so many of us get upset when the topic of stewardship or the subject of money is raised? Probably because our money reflects our value system more than almost any other area of our lives.

A well-known preacher once said that all he had to do was to look at one book in a person's home in order to tell the state of that person's spiritual life. Was it well worn and marked up or was it dust covered? All of us listening to him thought it was the Bible. But no, it was the checkbook. He reminded us that Jesus taught, "Where your treasure is, there your heart will be also" (Matthew 6:21). Actually, this passage is not so much about money as it is about attitudes.

Paul began this epistle to the Philippians discussing servanthood and spiritual maturity. Now he concludes the letter with a discussion of stewardship. In these verses we find at least five principles to guide us in our stewardship.

STEWARDSHIP IS SHARING

Stewardship is recognizing that all we have is God's. Therefore, it is to be available to others in time of need. Our resources are a trust from God. They are not given to us to gratify our selfish desires; they are given so that we can share with others. To the church at Corinth, Paul writes, "And now, brothers, we want you to know about the grace that God has given the Macedonian churches. Out of the most severe trial, their overflowing joy and their extreme poverty welled up in rich generosity" (2 Corinthians 8:1-2). The Philippians, who were Macedonians, were extremely poor, yet out of what little they had, they shared with Paul.

STEWARDSHIP IS CONTINUOUS

Paul recounts how the Philippians shared with him over and over again. It was not just a one-shot gift but an ongoing concern. In talking with mission executives, they tell me that they have very little trouble raising money for special projects. People will give toward a jeep or a hospital or some other project. What they have trouble with is raising ongoing support for missionaries. I find the same thing is true in churches. It is usually easy to raise money for a special project. It is more difficult to maintain the operating budget.

We readily respond to emotional appeals. We like to give when we think we are the ones who stand between the success or failure of a project. Stewardship, however, should not be based on emotions but on commitment. We need to make these commitments based on God's Word and His leading and then stick to them.

Whose Money Is It?

STEWARDSHIP IS GIVING TO GOD

When we give to our church or a mission agency or some other Christian work, we are not giving to an organization; we are giving to God. We give to God because He first gave to us.

In verse 17, Paul is saying that people were not giving to him but to God. When they gave, they were storing up treasures in heaven. The paradox of building treasures in heaven versus treasures on earth is that you cannot take anything with you, but you can send as much ahead as you like.

Some time back I read about a group of teenage girls who were committed to Christ and were quite interested in missions. In order to support a mission project, they decided to form a "Do Without" club. The idea was to raise money by giving up something. Most of the girls came from affluent homes and found it easy to give up various luxuries and give the money to missions.

But one of the girls, Margie, was quite poor. She went to her room and asked God to show her what she could do without. As she prayed, her pet spaniel came into the room. She remembered that their family doctor had wanted to buy him. Tears started to roll down her cheeks as she thought of parting with her dog, Bright. But she realized that God had given up His Son for her, and she resolved to sell the dog.

The next day Margie brought Bright to the doctor's house and sold him for $50 and gave the money to the missions fund. The doctor was quite happy at first to have the dog. He soon began to wonder, however, why Margie had sold him. The doctor called and talked with Margie. When he heard her story, he hung up in deep thought. The next morning as Margie was getting ready for school she heard scratching at the back door.

When she opened the door, Bright rushed in and jumped on her with joy. Margie saw a note fastened to the dog's collar. It read, "Your practical Christianity has done more for me than any sermon I've ever heard. Last night I offered what's left of my life to God. I'd like to join your "Do Without" club, and I'll begin by doing without Bright."

STEWARDSHIP IS ABUNDANT GIVING

Paul tells the Philippians that they have given more than enough. But how much is enough? What should our stewardship be? Each person needs to determine that with God. There are some principles in Scripture that we can apply to this question. The Bible distinguishes three levels of giving: tithes, offerings and sacrifices. Let us look at each of these a little closer.

The tithe, 10 percent of our income, is God's basic standard or starting point in stewardship. Tithes belong to God, and when we do not give God the tithe, we are robbing God every bit as much as if we took money from the offering plate. Now wait a minute, Preacher! That is a pretty strong statement. Where do you get that from? From Malachi 3:8—"Will a man rob God? yet you rob me. But you ask, 'How do we rob you?' In tithes and offerings."

Hold on now, Preacher. That was from the Old Testament. They were under the law. Christ did away with the law and we are under grace. That does not apply to us. I will refute that point in a minute. First, however, let me say that those people who raise that objection generally do not want to give more than the tithe. They have raised the objection so that they can give less. Yet it is interesting that whenever Jesus commented on a point of the law, He did not lower the demands, He raised them.

Whose Money Is It?

For example, the law taught against adultery; Jesus said we were not even to lust. The law said love your neighbor; Jesus said also love your enemy. The law said do not murder; Jesus said do not hate. The law said an eye for an eye; Jesus said turn the other cheek. Jesus summarized this by saying, "Do not think that I have come to abolish the Law or the Prophets; I have not come to abolish them but to fulfill them" (Matthew 5:17). If, therefore, you want to argue that tithing is part of the law, then we should do greater than the law, not just fulfilling the letter but the spirit of the law.

As I said earlier, tithing is for us because tithing transcends the law. It is God's plan for the ages. It is true that tithing is found in the law (Deuteronomy 12:6). But so is the commandment, "You shall not steal" (Exodus 20:15). Will you argue that this does not apply to us? Of course it does, because it transcends the law.

The tithe was considered God's portion hundreds of years before the law was ever given. We find Abraham giving the tithe to God (Genesis 14:20). We find Jacob giving the tithe to God (Genesis 28:22). In fact, Hebrews 7:9 notes that the tithe preceded the law.

In the New Testament we find Jesus confirming that the tithe was God's will. He said, "Woe to you, teachers of the law and Pharisees, you hypocrites! You give a tenth of your spices—mint, dill and cummin. But you have neglected the more important matters of the law—justice, mercy and faithfulness. You should have practiced the latter, without neglecting the former" (Matthew 23:23). What Jesus was saying was that the Pharisees were careful to tithe on every speck of income they received but neglected justice, mercy and faithfulness. Jesus said they were right to tithe but should also do the other. I have read every book I can find on stewardship, and I have yet to find an evangelical scholar who

103

argues that the New Testament calls for less than the tithe.

I will confess, I do have one problem with the tithe. Some people see it as the end of their stewardship. They reason, Ten percent for God and ninety percent for me. That's a pretty good deal. Even the government takes more than that from many of us. But the tithe was never meant to be the ceiling for our stewardship. It was meant to be the floor.

That brings us to the next level of stewardship: offerings. The word offering is used in three ways in the Bible. One use of the word is to refer to an animal that was to be offered on the altar. Another way offering is used in the Scripture is to refer to any gift. The third way, and the one we are interested in, is the free-will offering. Free-will offerings are gifts above and beyond the tithe given to show our love, appreciation and thanksgiving to God. They are acts of worship, often used for special projects or needs. In his epistles, the apostle Paul often talked about offerings for others (e.g., 2 Corinthians 8 and 9). The assumption was that the tithes were being used for the ministry of the local church, and the offerings were above-and-beyond gifts to help others in need.

The third level of stewardship is sacrifices. The word sacrifice is used two ways in Scripture. It is used to refer to an animal that was to be offered. It is also used to refer to giving what one cannot afford to give. In Luke's Gospel, we find an interesting account: "As he looked up, Jesus saw the rich putting their gifts into the temple treasury. He also saw a poor widow put in two very small copper coins. 'I tell you the truth,' he said, 'this poor widow has put in more than all the others. All these people gave their gifts out of their wealth; but she out of her poverty put in all she had

Whose Money Is It?

to live on'" (Luke 21:1-4).

It should be noted that gifts given in the treasury were above and beyond the tithe. The rich were giving significantly beyond the tithe, but Jesus tells us it was out of their excess. The widow, on the other hand, gave all she had. She sacrificed. From Jesus we learn that God values our gifts, not so much by their size but by their cost to us. Now, the interesting thing about sacrificing is that the person who truly sacrifices for God does not feel as though he is sacrificing.

Whenever I have an article published in a magazine, I give the royalty check to my wife to buy clothes for herself. A few months back I sold an article and signed the royalty check over to my wife. She needed a new pair of shoes, so it came at an opportune time. I soon learned that she used the money to buy some things for our children. She "sacrificed" her new shoes to buy some extras for our children which we ordinarily could not afford. She never thought of what she had done as a sacrifice—it was a delight to her. She loves her children. The person who loves God and sacrifices for His kingdom would often be surprised to hear us call it a sacrifice—that person calls it a delight. Love is never afraid of giving too much.

God is not interested in our money. He is interested in us. It is just that our money shows what we are interested in. A pastor was talking with a farmer one day. He asked the farmer, "If you had $200, would you give $100 to the Lord?" The farmer replied, "Of course I would." If you had two cows, would you give one to the Lord?" asked the pastor. "Sure," responded the farmer. "If you had two pigs," continued the pastor, "would you give one to the Lord?" "Now, that's not fair," complained the farmer. "You know I have two pigs."

I believe God wants every Christian to tithe. For you

that may be a sacrifice. My wife and I have tithed since we were married and we have a lifestyle based on 10 percent less income. But for the person who is not tithing, to start will mean a 10 percent cut in lifestyle. It is more difficult to give something up than never to have had it. I recognize that you may not totally agree with my position on tithing. It is not my responsibility to tell you what to do. Rather, let me encourage you to study God's Word and pray for His leading. I have shared my convictions; you must develop you own.

STEWARDSHIP IS TRUSTFULNESS

Paul assures the Philippian believers that God will meet their needs (v. 19). He tells them God will supply from His glorious riches through Christ Jesus. Jesus taught the same truth when He said, "Seek first his kingdom and his righteousness, and all these things [food and clothing] will be given to you as well" (Matthew 6:33). God promises to meet all our needs not all our greeds. When we give to God's glory, He cares for us to His glory.

FINAL GREETINGS

Paul concludes this letter by sending his greetings and the greetings of the Christians with him in Rome. Then he finishes where he began, with grace. Since God so freely gave to us, we should freely give of ourselves and our resources.

Paul has shared with us in this letter the secret of joy. We have seen that joy results from serving God and giving of ourselves, just as the Philippian church did. Joy comes from putting others first. Joy comes from biblical giving. Joy comes from sharing the gospel. Joy comes from being persecuted for righteousness sake. Joy comes from obedience. But primarily, joy

Whose Money Is It?

comes from our relationship with Jesus Christ.

DISCUSSION QUESTIONS

1. Why do you think we are so easily upset by talk of stewardship and money?
2. Read 2 Corinthians 8:7-9; 9:6-13. What principles of stewardship do you find in these verses?
3. Read Exodus 35:20-29. What is the motiviation for giving in this passage?
4. Do you agree or disagree with the author's position on tithing? If you disagree, what is your position? How do you support it? If you agree, why?
5. What have you seen as the central message of this epistle to the church at Philippi?